QUICK COOK

By the same Author

Summer Cook

The Daily Telegraph Book of
Breads, Cakes & Puddings

THANE PRINCE

QUICK COOK

Chatto & Windus
LONDON

First published in 1991 by
Chatto & Windus Ltd
20 Vauxhall Bridge Road
London SW1V 2SA

This edition published in 1994

A CIP catalogue record for this book is
available from the British Library.

ISBN 0 7011 6181 7

Design by Margaret Sadler
Photoset by Rowland Phototypesetting Ltd
Bury St Edmunds, Suffolk
Printed and bound in Great Britain by
Butler & Tanner Ltd, Frome and London

Contents

For Jade, Amber and Bob

Acknowledgements

I want to keep this list as short as possible. So thank you to my mother, for feeding me with such good food that I learnt about taste early in life, and to my sister Maureen, for helping me learn how to cook in a damp basement flat in Camden Town.

Thanks also to Gill Coleridge, who first suggested the idea of the book; to Wendy Jones, for her sensitive and appetizing illustrations; and to Linda Sonntag, who edited it with such enthusiasm.

Many others have helped me along the way: the Weekend team at *The Daily Telegraph*, chefs and friends whose recipes I've purloined, and readers who have written encouraging letters have all overwhelmed me with their generosity of spirit.

But most of my thanks are due to Trevor Grove, without whose help, encouragement, constructive criticism and friendship I would never have put pen to paper.

Introduction

I LOVE TO COOK: I find it relaxing and stimulating, soothing and creative. I also love to eat, but eating is only one of the many pleasures in life, and my aim in this book is to free the cook to enjoy them. In the recipes that follow, preparation time is always kept to a minimum. Cooking is made speedy, simple and pleasurable; and the result should look so colourful and appetizing and have such a delicious aroma you simply can't wait to sit down and eat it.

For me, a well cooked meal is close to being the perfect work of art. You can look at it, and talk admiringly of the skill needed to create it; and then you consume it. You don't have to hang it on the wall, listen to it, or worse still, wear it. With cooking, you can transform a necessary, everyday chore into a creative event, and end with a product that delights and sustains your family and friends.

Food is a fascinating subject. It gives a multitude of sensations, encompassing geography, history, science and language, reminding you of holidays past and stimulating interest in countries not yet explored. And today we have a seemingly endless variety of ingredients from which to choose. Air freight has meant that we have tropical fruits delivered year-round in perfect condition. Small cheese makers and herb farms flourish, specialist producers give us smoked foods, delicious corn-fed poultry, fresh pasta, virgin oils, spicy sausages, sun-dried tomatoes . . . meat comes cut and prepared in dozens of different ways. Any fish counter will offer a previously undreamed-of selection.

With this vast range of tastes has come the freedom to combine foods in new ways. Don't feel inhibited. Cooking is so much more fun if you trust your palate and your own experience. But when you come home tired and hungry after a working day, you won't want to try out a complex new recipe. The answer is to stock up with the wealth of wonderful foodstuffs at our disposal and to use this book to create a quick and delicious meal, so you spend more time relaxing with the family at the table and less time working in the kitchen.

No one ever taught me to cook – though I learned what good food tastes like from my mother – and none of the recipes in this book needs a knowledge of advanced cooking techniques. I am all in favour of short cuts and enlist help whenever I can. I use a food processor. I ask the fishmonger to skin and fillet fish and the butcher to bone and cut meat. I have a roomy store cupboard stocked with a wide range of dried and tinned goods, and I don't shun quality processed foods that merit use because they save valuable time. I treasure my efficient and well designed kitchen equipment.

I presume you are already armed with an adventurous palate. But before we go on to the recipes – which I promise are both *exciting and infallible* – here are a few words of advice on organizing the running of your kitchen for maximum efficiency.

The kitchen

I love my kitchen, and its comfortable atmosphere makes me feel good every time I start to cook. Cooking and eating are sensual pastimes, and a high-tech kitchen would inhibit me from experimenting, as my mind would be constantly on the mammoth clean-up it would require afterwards. Nevertheless, a kitchen should be organized for maximum efficiency.

□ If you are planning a new kitchen, put china, glasses, cutlery and dishwasher on one side of the sink, and food preparation including ingredients, saucepans, knives etc. on the other.

□ Make space on the work top for the labour-saving equipment you will be using all the time: the food processor, the kettle and the toaster. All the other wonderful gadgets can be stored in the cupboard or left in the shop, with the possible exception of a hand-held or free-standing electric mixer.

□ Good quality equipment repays the cook again and again. It is a joy to use, and its efficiency saves that most valuable of all commodities, time.

The oven

It is an interesting fact that the one piece of equipment you rely on most is often the one piece of equipment you didn't choose for yourself – the oven.

Using an oven without the instruction leaflet can be a problem. I have found severe shortcomings with some of the new wave continental ovens, especially when it comes to grilling. Kneeling on the floor, with flames and smoke coming from my pelvic-level grill, I battle with an ill designed grill pan balanced precariously on its plastic handle while hot fat spits on to the element. If you are buying a new stove, do make sure you get one with an eye-level grill.

If you have inherited someone else's oven, it is as well to check its efficiency and preheating time, and an oven thermometer provides an inexpensive way of avoiding failures on this score. Basic oven temperatures are as follows:

Low	150°C	300°F	Gas 2
Medium	180°C	360°F	Gas 4
High	220°C	425°F	Gas 7

The microwave

I find a microwave useful for defrosting, melting butter and chocolate, cooking sweetcorn, reheating coffee, cooking instant steamed puddings and making popcorn.

Following the recent concern over the ability of the microwave to cook food thoroughly, I recommend strongly that you read the instructions carefully and that you are aware of the wattage of your oven. If you have a low wattage oven, the cooking times will be longer. The Association of Domestic Appliances has published a leaflet with the catchphrase 'Cover it – Stir it – Rest it – Test it', which is sensible advice. I haven't worked out how you stir a plated meal you hope to reheat, so perhaps the phrase should also say 'Turn it'.

A word in favour of microwaves. Older children find them quite liberating to use for cooking their own meals. There is no saucepan to wash, and microwaves have the great virtue of switching themselves off. However, do make sure that whoever uses your oven does understand its operation.

Knives

Every cookbook stresses the importance of good sharp knives. The reason is simple: cutting with a sharp knife needs less pressure, so you save both time and effort, and the results are neater. I have a steel to hand while I am cooking and often sharpen my knives as I work, keeping the edges as keen as possible.

I use three basic knives, a 12 cm/5 inch vegetable knife, a 20 cm/8 inch general purpose knife and a large cook's chopping knife. Of course you can add many others: thin boning knives, flexible carving knives and wonderful two-handled chopping knives from Italy, but three good knives will see you through almost all eventualities.

☐ Keep knives in a drawer away from children. Knife blocks look good, but take up valuable space.

The food processor

I am completely devoted to my food processor. I, who use hardly any gadgets in my home, fell in love at first sight with this wonderful machine.

However, a food processor does have its shortcomings. It will make a soggy pulp of onions in seconds; it will form pastry into a sticky impossible mess of dough when your back is turned; it can reduce chopped meat to a paste while you reach for the pepper; and over-use can give a dreadful blandness to most foods.

You can't make meringues, or milk shakes, or beat cream or mash potatoes in a food processor, but you can do almost everything else.

Food processors make wonderful breads, cakes and pastry, they chop meat, nuts, fruit and vegetables, they grate carrots and Parmesan with ease, and they blend soups, sauces, choux pastes, potted meats, mayonnaise, pesto, dips and batters, making labour-intensive dishes the work of moments.

- ☐ Buy the best quality direct drive processor you can afford.
- ☐ Make sure that the size you have chosen is right for your needs.
- ☐ Keep it on the work surface, plugged in ready for use.
- ☐ Always add wet ingredients before dry when making batters.
- ☐ Fold flour into cake mixes with a few quick bursts of power.
- ☐ Don't bother to rinse when processing different ingredients for the same recipe.
- ☐ Use the processor half full when possible. It is less efficient when overloaded or underfilled.
- ☐ Remember the machine will do the work for you but not the thinking. Always watch carefully: they are very fast and processing time is often only a few seconds.
- ☐ You can't do away with a chopping board and knife, as regular sized pieces of food process best, so there is still initial preparation to be done by hand for some recipes.
- ☐ I have two bowls and two cutting blades. This enables me to overcome the biggest drawback, the constant washing of a fairly fiddly container.

Chopping boards

Against modern trends, I use wooden chopping boards, which I keep well scrubbed. Plastic boards are easier to clean, but I find them less sympathetic to the knife.

- ☐ To stop the board moving when you are using it, place a well wrung out damp cloth underneath.
- ☐ If you have a smooth work surface in your kitchen, roll pastry directly on this to avoid fiddling with pastry boards.

Cooking pans

When setting up your first kitchen, you will need a variety of saucepans and ovenproof dishes, but I have to say that the last thing I would choose is a carefully graded set of saucepans of any one make. I find the following essential:

- ☐ A huge pan for boiling pasta, making stock, cooking marmalade, chutneys and jams, and for mulling wine.

- ☐ Two large saucepans for vegetables, potatoes, rice etc.

- ☐ A medium sized, enamelled cast iron pan for making sauces, melting chocolate, and caramelizing sugar. Make sure your balloon whisk fits the contours of this saucepan well.

- ☐ A small non-stick pan for milk, custards and boiling cream.

- ☐ A 17.5 cm/7 inch non-stick omelette and pancake pan.

- ☐ A deep, straight sided frying pan with a lid.

- ☐ A heavy sauté pan.

- ☐ A large oval casserole.

- ☐ A medium round casserole.

- ☐ Various oval and round ovenproof gratin dishes.

- ☐ A fish kettle. This is endlessly useful, not only for cooking fish but for asparagus, for simmering all the Christmas puddings at once and for lending to neighbours!

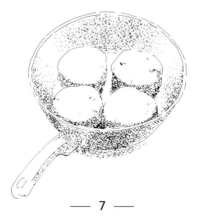

Shopping and storage

Throughout this book I have used ingredients which might at first seem expensive. My reason for this is simple. I consider time to be the scarcest commodity in most of our lives today, and I know that one way to save time is to spend a little extra on well prepared raw ingredients. You will find there is still a considerable saving over prepared meals, takeaways and eating out.

Buying raw ingredients carefully is probably the single most important step you can take towards good eating. Good quality food needs less preparation and less seasoning. The actual penny per pound difference will not be so great when wastage is considered.

With the growing demand for additive-free foods comes the responsibility for keeping foods that are low in preservatives fresh and fit for consumption. Food will start to warm up the minute it leaves the supermarket's chilled cabinet, so bring it home as quickly as possible – in an insulated bag if you have one – and unpack the perishable goods into the fridge/freezer before doing anything else.

- □ Don't buy ready cut vegetables, but by all means buy them ready washed: I can't see the point in carrying home mud on the potatoes.

- □ Buy tight-leaved salads – radiccio, fennel, chicory and Iceberg lettuce – to save washing time.

- □ Wash loose-leaved salads, spin dry and store in polythene bags in the fridge ready for use during the week.

- □ Always keep a few frozen vegetables for instant meals, or choose those with short preparation times, such as broccoli or courgettes.

- □ Buy boned, skinned fish fillets and ready trimmed meat, or ask your fishmonger or butcher to do these jobs for you.

- □ Buy bacon ready rinded.

- □ Store cooked and uncooked food separately to prevent cross-contamination.

- ☐ Use plastic boxes, or china bowls covered with plates, in preference to cling wrap.

- ☐ Unless vacuum-packed, remove fish and meat from plastic wrappings, wash under cold running water and store as above.

- ☐ Store cheese carefully wrapped in greaseproof paper in the fridge, but allow it to come to room temperature before serving.

- ☐ Dairy products pick up flavours, so store these, covered, away from strong tasting foods.

- ☐ Prepare grated cheese and breadcrumbs when time allows and store in airtight containers in the fridge.

- ☐ Jars of pastes – olive, tomato, mixed vegetable – and pots of pesto, chilli and garlic sauce can be added by the teaspoon to liven up simple dishes.

- ☐ Always keep a bottle of extra virgin olive oil to give an instant taste boost to grilled foods, vegetables and salads.

- ☐ Buy good quality stock cubes in a variety of flavours, or try the more expensive but delicious chilled stock.

- ☐ Continental cooked sausages, such as kabanos and frankfurters, only need heating through and add protein and taste to pasta sauces.

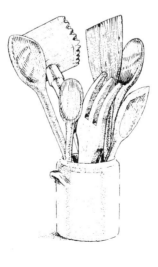

- ☐ Pulses deteriorate in keeping, so don't buy beans and peas in bulk unless you use them often.

- ☐ Fresh herbs, liberally sprinkled, give zest to any dish.

- ☐ Keep a roll of herb butter – made when time allows – in the freezer to slice on to grilled fish or meat or to make herb bread.

- ☐ Keep dried herbs and spices in a cupboard close to the stove. Wooden spice racks look delightful, but they collect dust and allow seasonings to spoil if kept in a hot bright place.

- ☐ Avoid dried chives, parsley, basil and chervil, as they have no resemblance to the fresh herbs. Thyme, sage, rosemary, marjoram and oregano dry well.

- ☐ Keep all the foods of one type – pastas, condiments, spreads etc. – on one shelf so you save time by going automatically to the right place.

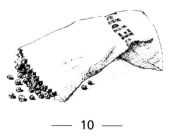

Chapter

1

15-minute meals

Putting a meal on the table quickly for a hungry family calls for all a cook's skill. Fortunately some of the best food is quickly and simply made, and these one-course, 15-minute meals show that you can deliver faster and better food than your local pizza delivery or takeaway service.

The recipes in this chapter can be infinitely varied to your own taste. If your store cupboard suggests alternative ingredients, then try them out. Inspiration often strikes when you are in a hurry.

I have not used potatoes and some forms of rice in this chapter, as they take longer than 15 minutes to cook, but if you have those extra few minutes, do serve them as an alternative to the bread or pasta I've suggested.

SCRAMBLED EGGS
with mushrooms and tarragon

serves 2
170 g/6 oz button mushrooms
2 tablespoons butter
6 large eggs
2 tablespoons cream
salt and freshly ground black pepper
**1 tablespoon fresh tarragon leaves,
   chopped**
4 large slices wholemeal toast, buttered

*Scrambled eggs have almost
disappeared from our rushed breakfast
tables. Served with granary toast, fresh
eggs make a delicious 'instant' meal.
For a more substantial dish add
mushrooms, smoked fish or minced
ham. In this version, the rich creaminess
of the eggs is complemented by the still
firm mushrooms and the distinctive
taste of tarragon.*

Wipe the mushrooms clean. Melt the
butter in a non-stick saucepan and fry
the mushrooms over a brisk heat until
they are golden brown. Meanwhile
make the toast. Beat the eggs with the
cream and season with a little salt and
plenty of freshly ground pepper. Tip the
eggs into the pan with the mushrooms
and cook over a moderate heat, stirring
often to break the eggs into large flakes.
Just before they are set add the chopped
tarragon.
  Serve with toast triangles.

SCRAMBLED EGGS
with sun-dried tomatoes & basil

serves 2
6 sun-dried tomatoes, chopped
1 tablespoon butter
6 large eggs, beaten
2 tablespoons cream
salt and freshly ground black pepper
2–3 sprigs fresh basil, roughly torn
4 large slices wholemeal toast, buttered

*Sun-dried tomatoes can be quite salty,
so remember to adjust the seasoning
accordingly. Basil leaves are always
torn rather than chopped to retain as
much flavour as possible. You could
replace the tomatoes and basil with:
minced ham and a teaspoon of
mustard; grated Cheddar cheese with
chives; or smoked salmon and chervil.*

Soak the tomatoes in a little boiling
water for 5 minutes, then drain well.
Make the toast. Melt the butter in a
non-stick saucepan. Beat the eggs with
the cream, salt and pepper. Add the
eggs to the pan and stir, breaking them
into large flakes over a moderate heat.
Just before they are set, stir in the
tomatoes and basil. Serve with the toast
triangles.

OMELETTE ARNOLD BENNETT

per person
115 g/4 oz smoked haddock
2 tablespoons double cream
cayenne pepper to taste
2 large eggs
1 tablespoon cold water
salt and freshly ground black pepper
1 teaspoon butter

Omelettes are well known as fast food. Infinitely variable, the basic recipe calls for fresh eggs, a little butter and salt. The traditional way of cooking this omelette is on a tin plate under the grill – no extra washing up!
You could replace the haddock and cream with: grated cheese and chopped tomatoes; fried mushrooms and fresh herbs; or courgettes, fried in butter with garlic.

Poach the haddock in water for 4–5 minutes. Drain, remove the skin, and bone and flake the fish. Stir in the cream and cayenne pepper. Beat the eggs with the water and salt and pepper.

Omelettes need quick cooking, so heat a non-stick frying pan well before putting in the butter. It will melt immediately. Pour in the eggs. The sides of the omelette will set immediately, so pull them into the middle and let the raw eggs flow around the pan. When the omelette is nearly cooked, pour in the fish mixture and allow it to heat, then slide it on to a warm serving dish.

COURGETTE & CHICKPEA GRATIN

serves 4
1 tin chickpeas, drained
190 g/7 oz chopped tinned tomatoes,
    plus 1 tablespoon tomato purée
1 teaspoon chopped fresh thyme or
    oregano leaves
1 tablespoon olive oil
340 g/12 oz small firm courgettes, sliced
1 fat clove of garlic, chopped
salt, pepper
115 g/4 oz grated cheese

Grilled cheese is not only appealing to the eye, it gives any dish extra taste and protein. Vegetarians could use non-animal rennet cheese for this gratin. Hearty eaters could use two tins of chickpeas and increase the courgettes to 450 g/1 lb.

Put the chickpeas, the tomatoes and the herbs in a saucepan and bring to the boil. Turn the heat down and simmer these together while you prepare the courgettes. Put the grill on to heat.

Heat the oil in a pan and stir-fry the courgettes with the garlic, until crisp-tender, about 4–5 minutes. Mix the chickpeas with the courgettes, correct the seasoning and pour everything into a gratin dish. Level the surface and sprinkle over the grated cheese.

Cook under the grill until the cheese bubbles and is golden brown. Serve with lots of fresh bread. Some chilli flakes can be added to the tomato sauce for lovers of hot food.

POACHED SCALLOPS
with tarragon butter sauce & fresh pasta

serves 2
225 g/8 oz fresh pasta
8 large scallops with coral
½ glass water
1 glass white wine
salt and freshly ground black pepper
1 shallot, chopped
60 g/2 oz butter, diced
1 tablespoon chopped fresh tarragon leaves

Scallops are so often spoiled by overcooking. They need to be briefly cooked – for as little as 60 seconds if thinly sliced – until just opaque.

Scallops are obviously a must for quick meals.

Bring a large saucepan of water to the boil and cook the pasta for about 3 minutes until al dente. Slice each scallop into 2 pieces. Bring the water and wine to a low boil, add a little salt and pepper and poach the scallops with their corals for 2–3 minutes until just opaque. Remove and keep warm. Drain the cooked pasta, transfer to a warmed dish and keep warm.

Put the shallot into the cooking liquid and boil briskly until reduced to one third. Turn the heat to low and beat in the butter, whisking until the sauce is combined. Remove from the heat and stir in the tarragon and scallops. Pour the sauce over the pasta and serve.

GRILLED FISH
with piquant sauce

serves 4
4 fillets of white fish: haddock, cod, coley or whiting
salt and pepper
1 tablespoon virgin olive oil

for the sauce
60 g/2 oz butter
1–2 cloves of garlic, crushed
2 tablespoons capers, chopped
juice of 1 lemon
2–3 anchovy fillets, chopped

Choose fish fillets that are even in size to achieve the best result. Frozen fillets can be thawed in a microwave according to the manufacturer's instructions.

Heat the grill to hot. For easy cleaning, line the base of the grill pan with foil. Season the fish fillets and brush with the olive oil.

Melt the butter in a saucepan and cook until beginning to brown, add the garlic and stir-fry for 1 minute. Remove the pan from the heat and stir in the capers, lemon juice and anchovy fillets, mixing well. Season with black pepper but add salt sparingly.

When the grill is hot, cook the fish fillets for 3–5 minutes each side until just cooked through. Serve with the piquant sauce, a green vegetable, such as frozen petit pois, and hot bread to mop up the sauce.

POACHED FISH
with tomato chilli sauce

serves 4
4 fillets fish (skinned, boned cod is good)
2 tablespoons olive oil
1 onion, chopped
1 plump clove of garlic, chopped
salt and freshly ground black pepper
1 glass water
1 medium tin chopped tomatoes
1 small chilli, sliced, or to taste
juice and rind of half a lemon
1 teaspoon arrowroot (optional)
2 tablespoons chopped fresh parsley
**2 tablespoons chopped fresh coriander
  leaves**

*Serve this dish with basmati rice: see
packet for instructions.*

Start by putting the rice on to cook.

Heat the oil in a frying pan and cook
the onion and garlic for 2–3 minutes
until transparent. Slice the fish into
strips 2.5 cm/1 inch wide and place
them in the pan on top of the
vegetables. Season with salt and pepper
and pour over the water. Bring to the
boil, cover and cook for 4–5 minutes
until the fish is just cooked.

Carefully remove the fish strips from
the pan, transfer to a serving dish, and
keep warm. Put the tomatoes, chilli,
lemon rind and juice in the frying pan
and turn the heat up high. Boil the
sauce, stirring, until reduced to half its
volume. Check the seasoning and
correct as necessary. If you prefer a
thickened sauce, slake a teaspoon of
arrowroot in 2 tablespoons water and
add to the sauce, stirring constantly.
Cook for 2 minutes, then stir in the
fresh herbs. Put the fish back into the
sauce and serve with the cooked
basmati rice.

PAN-STEAMED FISH CUTLETS
with creamy leek sauce

serves 4
**4 fish cutlets, e.g. salmon, haddock, brill,
  swordfish**
2 tablespoons butter
2 leeks, cleaned and sliced
salt, black pepper
**1 glass white wine, or 1 glass water plus
  2 tablespoons wine vinegar**
150 ml/¼ pint double cream
1–2 tablespoons chopped dill

*Serve this dish with pasta or basmati
rice.*

Melt the butter in a frying pan and
cook the leeks for 3–4 minutes. Season
the fish cutlets and place on top of the
leeks. Pour over the wine and bring the
mixture to a gentle boil. Cover and
cook the fish for 6–7 minutes until just
cooked.

Remove the cutlets to a heated dish
and keep warm. Turn up the heat and
boil to reduce the sauce by two-thirds.
Add the cream and bring to the boil.
Correct the seasoning, stir in the
chopped dill and pour over the fish.

FRESH PASTA

The wonderful thing about fresh pasta is that it's quick to cook and so delicious in itself that sauces can be very simple. You can make an 'instant' sauce by tossing pasta in rich green olive oil and Parmesan cheese, or in pesto, or tomato or black olive paste. Serve it with hot crusty bread, a simple salad, and a bottle of wine, and you have a meal fit for a king.

On average 450 g/1 lb fresh pasta will serve 4 people, and usually needs about 3 minutes' cooking in boiling salted water.

PASTA & KABANOS
with chilli tomato sauce

serves 4
450 g/1 lb fresh pasta
2 tablespoons olive oil
1 onion, chopped
1–2 cloves garlic, chopped
1 tin chopped tomatoes
2 kabanos sausages, chopped
1–2 small dried chillies
salt and black pepper
chopped fresh parsley

Cook the pasta in a large pan and drain.

Heat the oil in a frying pan and fry the onion and garlic until soft and beginning to brown. Add the tomatoes, sausage, chillies and seasoning. Simmer the sauce until thick, then stir in the parsley and serve with fresh noodles.

PASTA
with soured cream, tuna & chive sauce

serves 4
450 g/1 lb fresh pasta
1 tablespoon butter
1 tin tuna, drained and flaked
300 ml/½ pint soured cream
salt and ground black pepper
a large bunch of chives, chopped
freshly grated Parmesan cheese

Cook the pasta in a large pan and drain. Melt the butter in the pan and toss the pasta in it. Stir the tuna, cream and seasoning into the pasta, toss in the chives and serve at once with Parmesan cheese.

PASTA
with bacon, black olives & sun-dried tomatoes

serves 4
450 g/1 lb fresh pasta
170 g/6 oz bacon, rinded and sliced into strips
1 onion, chopped
1 clove garlic, crushed
60 g/2 oz sun-dried tomatoes, chopped
60 g/2 oz stoned black olives, chopped
salt and black pepper
fresh coriander, chopped

Cook the pasta in a large pan and drain.

Soften the bacon in a frying pan and when the fat runs, put in the onion and garlic. Cook, stirring often, until the bacon is crisp and the onion browned. Stir in the tomatoes and olives and toss the pasta in this sauce, seasoning to taste. Sprinkle with coriander.

Pasta
with ham, Parmesan & cream sauce

serves 4
450 g/1 lb fresh pasta
1 tablespoon butter
2 egg yolks, beaten
150 ml/¼ pint single cream
4 heaped tablespoons freshly grated
**   Parmesan cheese**
115 g/4 oz sliced ham, shredded
fresh parsley, chopped
salt and black pepper

Cook the pasta in a large pan and drain.

Melt the butter and toss in the hot pasta. Beat the eggs with the cream and the cheese and toss the pasta in this; the heat of the pasta will cause the sauce to thicken. Finally toss in the ham slices and parsley. Season and serve at once.

Pasta
with smoked fish & lemon cream sauce

serves 4
450 g/1 lb fresh pasta
300 ml/½ pint double cream
rind and juice of a large lemon
salt and freshly ground black pepper
170 g/6 oz skinned and boned smoked
**   fish (salmon, trout or mackerel), sliced**
fresh dill, chopped
freshly grated Parmesan cheese

Cook the pasta in a large pan and drain.

In a saucepan bring the cream to the boil. Stir in the lemon juice and seasoning and simmer for 2–3 minutes. Stir in the fish and heat through. Place the pasta in a heated serving dish and pour the sauce in the centre. Sprinkle generously with dill and hand the cheese separately.

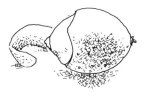

STIR-FRIED CHICKEN & VEGETABLES
with Chinese noodles

serves 4
3 medium boneless chicken breast fillets
1 tablespoon soy sauce
2 tablespoons oil
2 spring onions, sliced
1 clove garlic, chopped
a selection of the following vegetables, sliced or chopped into batons: courgette, red pepper, miniature corn cobs, mangetout, broccoli, Chinese leaf, mushrooms, beansprouts
2 tablespoons hoisin sauce (Chinese barbecue sauce)
1 cup stock
3 sheets Chinese noodles
1 teaspoon sesame oil
2 tablespoons sesame seeds
2 tablespoons soy sauce
1 teaspoon cornflour, slaked with 1–2 tablespoons water

Slice the chicken into strips 1 cm/½ inch wide and 7.5 cm/3 inches long, and sprinkle with soy sauce. Put a saucepan of water on to boil for the noodles.

Put the noodles in the water and turn off the heat. Cover the pan and allow them to sit for 6 minutes.

Heat a wok or large frying pan and then put in the oil. Swirl it around the pan to coat the sides and then put in the chicken strips and stir-fry for 2–3 minutes. Remove the chicken to a warm serving dish leaving the oil in the pan.

Put the onion and garlic in the pan, stir, and add the remaining vegetables except the beansprouts. Stir and fry until crisp and tender. Return the chicken to the wok, stir in the hoisin sauce and the stock, and simmer for 2–3 minutes. Add the beansprouts.

Drain and toss the noodles with sesame oil, sesame seeds and soy sauce, and keep hot. Stir the slaked cornflour into the chicken and boil for 1–2 minutes to thicken and cook the flour. Serve at once with the noodles.

PAN-FRIED LIVER
with orange & green peppercorn sauce

serves 4
450 g/1 lb lambs liver, thinly sliced
1 tablespoon olive oil
1 cup fresh orange juice
1 tablespoon marmalade
1 teaspoon crushed green peppercorns
salt and black pepper
150 ml/¼ pint stock
½ teaspoon arrowroot

This recipe is so simple and delicious that I'm delighted every time I cook it. In fact it's so good that offal-haters forget they are eating liver. Serve it with basmati rice and a lightly cooked green vegetable such as spinach or broccoli.

Heat the oil in a frying pan and fry the liver briskly, a few slices at a time, for about 2 minutes on either side. The liver should be browned on the outside but still pink in the middle. Remove the slices to a heated serving dish and keep warm while you make the sauce.

Pour the orange juice into the frying pan and, stirring well, add the marmalade, peppercorns, seasoning and stock. Boil the sauce rapidly, stirring constantly, to reduce by one third. Thicken the sauce with the arrowroot slaked with 2 tablespoons cold water. Pour the sauce over the liver and serve at once.

BEST-EVER HAMBURGERS

makes 4
450 g/1 lb minced beef
1 small onion
1 fat clove garlic
2 tablespoons double cream
1 tablespon parsley
salt and pepper
4 muffins

The homemade version of this ubiquitous high street food is delicious and also scores highly for being quick to cook and easy to eat.

I make burgers from ground beef, lamb or pork. I use a dry, ridged heavy iron griddle available from most kitchen departments to cook not only these meat patties but steaks also. Having a horror of the burger bun I always tuck these best-ever hamburgers inside a toasted muffin.

In a food processor, chop the onion and garlic in the cream. Add the beef, parsley and seasoning and continue to process, in short bursts, until everything is just mixed. Turn the meat out on to a board and form into 4 patties about 10 cm/4 inches across and 2.5 cm/1 inch deep.

Heat a griddle or heavy frying pan and when hot, put on the burgers. While they are cooking, toast and butter the muffins and prepare any accompanying salad. Cook the burgers for about 3 minutes each side, according to personal taste, and serve in the prepared muffins.

LAMB, MINT & YOGHURT PATTIES

makes 4
450 g/1 lb minced lamb
1 onion
1 fat clove garlic
2 tablespoons natural yoghurt
small bunch fresh mint
salt and black pepper

Process and cook the ingredients as for Best-ever hamburgers, see left. Serve with a crisp salad in pockets of toasted pitta bread.

PORK PATTIES
with apple & sage

makes 4
450 g/1 lb minced pork
1 onion
1 small eating apple
1 small egg, beaten
small bunch sage leaves
salt and pepper

Follow the method for Best-ever hamburgers (left). These fruity pork burgers are good with crisp chips and a fresh tomato sauce.

WARM BACON SALAD

serves 4
**225 g/8 oz streaky bacon, rinded and
  sliced**
2 tablespoons oil
115 g/4 oz sliced bread, cubed
1 bulb of fennel
endive, spinach or small salad leaves
1 head radiccio
1 ripe avocado
salt and pepper
lemon juice to taste

*Simplest of the newly fashionable
'warm salads' is the traditional bacon
and curly endive. I like to extend this
by adding cubes of crisp fried bread,
avocado, fennel and a variety of leaves.*

Put the bacon into a heavy pan and
cook until the fat runs, then turn up the
heat to crisp the bacon. Remove from
the pan, put in the oil and fry the bread
cubes until crisp.

Meanwhile, slice the fennel, tear the
salad into medium pieces and chop the
avocado roughly. Arrange everything in
a large bowl and sprinkle with salt and
pepper. Put the bacon back into the
frying pan and reheat it. Pour the bread,
bacon and hot oil over the salad,
sprinkle with lemon juice and serve.

WARM SALMON SALAD
with pine nuts

serves 4
**450 g/1 lb skinned and boned salmon
  fillet**
2 tablespoons olive oil
2 tablespoons pine nuts
1 tablespoon balsamic vinegar
selection of tiny salad leaves

*Buy salmon filleted and skinned to save
time with this dish. If you don't have
balsamic vinegar, use a wine vinegar or
a little fresh lemon juice.*

Heat the oil in a non-stick frying pan
and slice the salmon into 2.5 cm/1 inch
cubes. Pan-fry the fish in the hot oil for
3–4 minutes, until just cooked through.
Arrange the salad leaves on four plates
and divide the fish between them.
Quickly fry the nuts in the pan until
lightly browned and then pour them
and the oil over the fish. Sprinkle each
salad with a few drops of vinegar and
serve at once with fresh bread.

Hand extra oil and vinegar
separately.

GRILLED GOATS CHEESE SALAD
with spinach & walnut oil

per person
1 small slice goats cheese
spinach leaves, washed and torn into
  pieces
freshly ground black pepper and salt
1–2 tablespoons walnut oil
1 teaspoon sherry vinegar

Heat the grill and arrange the salad
leaves on plates. Grill the slices of
cheese, on foil for easier handling, for
about 3 minutes each side, and place on
the salad. Sprinkle with walnut oil and
vinegar. Serve with hot crispy bread.

TUNA & MIXED BEAN SALAD

serves 4
2 tins drained red kidney or butter beans
190 g/7 oz tinned tuna in oil
1 large Spanish or 2 medium red skinned
  onions, sliced into rings
2 tablespoons good olive oil
1 tablespoon wine vinegar
salt and black pepper
chopped flat leaf parsley or fresh
  coriander
60 g/2 oz black olives

*This Italian salad is most usually made
with large white butter beans, but I like
to use a mixture of whatever tinned
beans I have to hand. Use a mild variety
of onion and a full flavoured olive oil. If
you have large appetites double the
amount of tuna used.*

Drain the beans well and put into a
serving bowl. Flake the tuna and add to
the beans along with the oil in the can.
Stir in the onions. Mix the olive oil and
vinegar together and pour over the
salad. Season with salt and lots of
freshly ground black pepper and then
toss everything together. Sprinkle over
the chopped fresh herbs, decorate with
the olives and serve with crusty bread:
Italian ciabatta would be delicious.

Pizza

1 vacuum packed pizza base per person
**1 tin chopped tomatoes, or passata, or
  tomato purée**
**grated cheese or sliced mozzarella
  cheese**
tuna fish chunks
sliced peperoni
chopped ham
anchovies
olives
sardines
sliced mushrooms
peppers
onions
ready-made ratatouille
oregano, fresh or dried
olive oil
salt, black pepper
chilli peppers

*Here is the homemade answer to the
takeaway pizza: the individually created
designer pizza. Put the oven on to heat,
set out the toppings and each person
can create their own favourite. Those
taking too long may not quite catch the
15 minutes deadline, but the result is
bound to be delicious. The use of
prepared pizza bases saves the time
needed for fresh dough to rise twice.*

Heat the oven to 220°C/425°F/Gas 7.
Place the pizza bases on a baking sheet
and drizzle on a little oil. Starting with
tomato and ending with cheese, build
up the toppings to taste. Sprinkle the
pizzas with herbs, season with salt and
pepper and bake for 10 minutes until
the cheese bubbles. Serve at once.

Peppery Mackerel Pâté
with toast & crunchy salad

serves 4
**225 g/8 oz peppered smoked mackerel
  fillets**
115 g/4 oz cream cheese
2 tablespoons lemon juice

for the salad
2 heads of blanched chicory, sliced
1 large orange, peeled and sliced
3 ribs of celery, sliced
1 green apple, chopped
1 small red onion, chopped

for the dressing
1 tablespoon olive oil
1 tablespoon fresh orange juice
½ teaspoon honey
salt, freshly ground black pepper

*Smoked fish pâtés are so simple and
economical to make at home you will
wonder why you ever used the bought
versions. As this mackerel pâté is very
rich I like to serve it with a crunchy
salad and hot granary toast.*

*Similar pâtés can be made using other
types of fish: smoked trout, smoked
salmon trimmings, tinned tuna, fresh
salmon. Season each type according to
personal taste, remembering that
smoked fish is often salty.*

For the pâté, put the skinned fish fillets
into a food processor, add the cheese
and lemon juice and process until
smooth. Pile the pâté into a serving dish
and chill while you assemble the salad.

Toss the salad ingredients together in
a bowl. Combine the ingredients for the
dressing by shaking together in a jar.
Pour the dressing over the salad and
serve with the pâté and hot toast.

Fried cheese sandwiches

per person
2 slices brown bread, buttered
60–85 g/2–3 oz mature Cheddar cheese,
  thinly sliced
olive oil for frying
1 clove garlic, crushed

*Fried cheese sandwiches served with a
bowl of tomato soup are a favourite
late-night snack of mine. While the
soup comes from a tin (or use
homemade frozen soup, p. 134), mature
Cheddar and good wholemeal bread lift
this meal to great heights.*

Make the sandwich in the usual
manner, and cut into triangles. Heat the
oil in a frying pan with the garlic. When
the oil is hot, remove the garlic and fry
the sandwiches until golden brown each
side and the cheese runs. Serve at once.

For extra luxury, try spreading the
bread with wholegrain mustard or
mango chutney.

A junior version of these sandwiches
can be made using high fibre white
bread, processed cheese or Edam, and
frying in sunflower oil.

Creole submarine sandwich

serves 4
4 thin slices leg of pork
Creole seasoning
4 large bread rolls, wholegrain are best
butter
Iceberg lettuce
1 small red onion, sliced
oil for frying
150 ml/¼ pint soured cream

*Submarine sandwiches hail from the
United States and are named for the
shape of the roll in which they are
made. America has a range of hot
sandwiches that make good quick
meals. This particular one features thin
slices of pork, fried very quickly in a
non-stick pan or on a griddle. The
recipe for the Creole seasoning can be
found on p. 174 and is a good standby
for instant flavour on chops and fish
fillets.*

If you are using a griddle, put it on the
stove to heat. Season the pork slices
liberally with the spice and clip the
edges so they lie flat in the pan. Butter
the bread rolls and fill each one with
some shredded lettuce leaves and red
onion. Fry the pork slices either on the
griddle or in a non-stick pan with a very
little oil for 2–3 minutes each side. Put
one slice into each roll, top with a
spoonful of soured cream and serve at
once.

BACON, AVOCADO, LETTUCE & TOMATO SANDWICHES (B.A.L.T.)

per person
6 rashers streaky bacon, rinded and thinly sliced
3 slices white bread, toasted and buttered
1–2 tablespoons mayonnaise
½ large beef tomato, thinly sliced
¼ ripe avocado, sliced
2–3 lettuce leaves, shredded

This is the all-time favourite American sandwich. I like white toast, mayonnaise, and for pure indulgence I add avocado. The bacon must be crisp. The tomatoes firm and the lettuce a variety with plenty of crunch.

Fry or grill the bacon until crisp.

Meanwhile, make the toast and start to assemble the sandwich. Place one slice of toast on a plate and spread on a little mayonnaise. Then put on the tomato and avocado, followed by another slice of buttered toast. Spread the top of this slice with the remaining mayonnaise, and pile on the shredded lettuce. Next add the crisply grilled bacon, and finally the last slice of buttered toast. Don't forget to season as you go!

Slice the sandwich into four triangles and, for true authenticity, serve with potato crisps and a dill pickle.

PO' BOYS

makes 4
450 g/1 lb firm fish fillets, boned, skinned and cut into 2.5 cm/1 inch cubes
seasoned flour
1 egg, beaten, and well seasoned with salt and pepper
fresh white breadcrumbs
150 ml/¼ pint mayonnaise
1 small onion, quartered
3–4 pickled miniature gherkins
1 tablespoon capers
1 fresh French stick, cut into four
shredded lettuce
oil for frying
lemon wedges

Po' boys are the native sandwich of New Orleans. There as here, oysters were once the food of the poor, and fried oysters made a tasty sandwich filling. However, any type of fish can be used as long as it is free of bones and skin and sufficiently chunky not to get lost in its breadcrumb coating. Frozen breaded scampi are good served in this way.

Toss the fish in the seasoned flour and then in the egg, and then the breadcrumbs. Leave the coated cubes to dry a little, spread out on a board, while you prepare the sauce.

In a food processor mix the mayonnaise, onion, gherkins and capers until roughly chopped. Slice open the four pieces of French bread and put on a serving dish with some shredded lettuce piled into each one. Fry the cubes of fish in the hot oil for 4–5 minutes until crisp and golden brown. Drain and divide among the rolls. Put 1–2 tablespoons of sauce on top of the fish and then put on the top of the roll. Serve with lemon wedges.

BRUSCHETTA WITH MOZZARELLA, PARMA HAM AND TOMATOES

serves 4
4 thick slices rustic white bread
1 clove garlic, crushed
3–4 tablespoons olive oil
salt and black pepper
4 slices Parma ham
1 beef tomato, sliced
fresh basil leaves
225 gm/8 oz Mozzarella cheese, sliced

This Italian inspired sandwich is best made with thickish slices of rustic bread. Use a pungent green olive oil, fine slices of Parma ham and fresh basil leaves.

Heat the grill.
Toast the bread lightly. Mix the crushed garlic into the oil, brush the slices with the mixture and season with salt and freshly ground black pepper.
Lay a slice of ham on each bruschetta and then one or two slices of tomato and a torn basil leaf. Cover with sliced Mozzarella.
Return the toast to the heated grill until the cheese bubbles. Serve with a crisp lettuce and cucumber salad.

WALDORF SALAD

serves 4
4 medium red skinned apples
1 small head celery
115 gm/4 oz mature cheddar cheese (optional)
4 heaped tablespoons mayonnaise
4 tablespoons soured cream
salt and pepper
85 gm/3 oz roughly chopped walnuts

In a memorable episode of Fawlty Towers, John Cleese explained to a bemused guest that he was unable to have the salad he'd ordered as Waldorfs were not in season. A pity, as this crunchy salad makes a delicious light meal.

Core and dice the apples, chop the celery and cube the cheese if used.
Beat the mayonnaise with the cream and season with salt and plenty of freshly ground black pepper. Toss the prepared ingredients with this dressing.
Serve with granary bread.

Chapter
2

30-minute meals

THESE MENUS FORM the heart of the book, and bring supper to the table in 30 minutes. Good enough to serve to friends, this food will make every meal you eat a delicious treat, all the more so as it is ready so quickly.

Often I advise leaving the pudding to cook while you enjoy the main course, but sometimes it is necessary to start preparing the dessert first to allow the longest possible time for it to set or chill.

Just because these delicious meals are fast to prepare does not mean that you must rush through them: relax and enjoy the food.

MENU 1

BLACKENED CHICKEN PASTA
with tomatoes & fresh coriander

MIXED LEAF SALAD

GREEK YOGHURT
with macerated summer fruit

serves 4

BLACKENED CHICKEN PASTA
with tomatoes & fresh coriander

4 chicken breasts, boned and skinned
2–3 tablespoons Creole spice (see p. 174)
1 scant tablespoon oil
450 g/1 lb fresh pasta
300 ml/½ pint double cream
salt and black pepper to taste
3 large tomatoes, diced
a handful of fresh coriander or parsley,
chopped

This delicious chicken and pasta dish has its roots in the Creole cooking of the southern United States. If you have time, sprinkle the spice on the chicken in the morning and leave it in the fridge. I have used lots of fresh coriander to give colour and a wonderful fresh green taste, but you could easily substitute parsley or chopped spring onions.

A simple mixed leaf salad, served after the pasta, should be dressed with a light coating of oil and vinegar to give a contrast to the rich spicy sauce on the pasta.

As early as possible, sprinkle the washed chicken breasts with the spice. When you are ready to cook, put a large saucepan of water on for the pasta and put a large serving dish in the oven to heat.

Heat a little oil in a large frying pan and cook the chicken, turning as needed for about 10 minutes, until cooked through and golden brown.

Cook the pasta.

Remove the chicken from the pan and keep warm. Pour the cream into the pan and heat up to boiling point, stirring all the time to incorporate any spice that has stuck to the bottom of the pan. Simmer to reduce slightly, and check the seasoning.

Drain the pasta, tip into the serving dish, pour over the cream and toss lightly. Slice the chicken breasts into strips and pile these, the chopped tomatoes and the coriander on to the dish.

Serve at once.

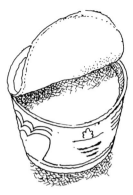

GREEK YOGHURT
with macerated summer fruit

600 ml/ 1 pint thick Greek style yoghurt
450 g/1 lb mixed summer fruit
about 2 tablespoons caster sugar, or to
   taste
1–2 tablespoons brandy or port

*Fresh fruit is ideal, but thawed frozen
fruit will do as well. If possible, thaw
the fruit during the day in the
refrigerator.*

Wash the fruit, remove stems, leaves or
hulls, and mash lightly with a fork.
Sprinkle over the sugar, and then the
port or brandy. Leave this to soak.
   When you are ready to serve, divide
the yoghurt between four dessert glasses
and spoon over the fruit and juice.

MENU 2

PASTA WITH AUBERGINE, GARLIC & SUN-DRIED TOMATOES

ORANGE & CHICORY SALAD

FRESH PEACH & CINNAMON SPONGE PUDDING

FRESH CREAM

serves 4

PASTA WITH AUBERGINE, GARLIC & SUN-DRIED TOMATOES

3 tablespoons good olive oil
1 large onion, sliced
2–3 cloves garlic, peeled and crushed
450 g/1 lb aubergine, cut into 1 cm/½ inch dice
6–8 dried tomato halves, or 3 large fresh tomatoes, sliced
fresh thyme
salt and pepper to taste
½ glass white wine (optional)
400 g/14 oz dried pasta such as fusilli or penne
5–6 tablespoons freshly grated Parmesan cheese

Wonderful pasta sauces can be made very simply and this one is perfect for vegetarians. I don't worry about salting the aubergines to sweat them if they are fresh, as they will be cooked quickly. Dried tomatoes in oil are soft and ready to use, or you could substitute large ripe beef tomatoes, which changes the taste and texture slightly. Both are delicious.

Heat the oil in a saucepan, and over a brisk heat fry the onion until it softens, then add the garlic and fry for 1 minute. Add the aubergine and cook, stirring until covered in oil and beginning to brown. Put in the tomatoes, thyme, salt and pepper. Pour in the wine, stir well, turn the heat down to low and cook for 5 minutes, stirring often.

Cook and drain the pasta and place in a heated serving dish. Pour over the sauce, sprinkle on the Parmesan cheese and serve with Orange and chicory salad, opposite.

ORANGE & CHICORY SALAD

2 large oranges, peeled and sliced
2 heads Belgian chicory, sliced
1 teaspoon sherry vinegar
1 tablespoon olive oil
salt and pepper

Arrange the orange with the chicory on a plate and sprinkle over the vinegar and oil. Season to taste.

FRESH PEACH & CINNAMON SPONGE PUDDING

4 medium peaches

for the sponge
115 g/4 oz soft margarine
115 g/4 oz light muscavado sugar
2 medium eggs
115 g/4 oz wholemeal flour
1½ teaspoons baking powder
1½ teaspoons ground cinnamon

for the topping
1 tablespoon light muscavado sugar
1 teaspoon cinnamon

This deliciously light and juicy pudding takes moments to prepare and can be cooking while you eat the pasta.

Cover the peaches with boiling water for 60 seconds and skin them. Chop roughly into 1 cm/½ inch cubes. For the sponge, mix the ingredients together, then stir in peach cubes. Pour the mixture into a greased ovenproof dish.

Mix together the sugar and cinnamon for the topping and sprinkle this over the sponge. Bake in a preheated oven, at 200°C/400°F/Gas 6, for 25–30 minutes. Serve with cream.

Menu 3

Cold pasta salad
with dilled mayonnaise & seafood

Tomato & watercress salad

Strawberries in champagne

serves 4

Cold pasta salad
with dilled mayonnaise & seafood

285 g/10 oz rice-shaped pasta
1 egg yolk
1 teaspoon Dijon mustard
1 scant tablespoon wine vinegar
150 ml/¼ pint mixed olive oil and light
  vegetable oil
a handful fresh dill
1–2 tablespoons single cream
salt and pepper
340 g/12 oz cold cooked fish, e.g.
  prawns, salmon, smoked trout
4 spring onions, chopped
watercress and tomatoes, to serve

This is a menu for a special occasion featuring prawns, smoked fish and fizzy wine, if not champagne. The homemade mayonnaise gives a wonderful flavour to the rice-shaped pasta.

You can use this basic recipe with many variations: cold chicken and tarragon can be substituted for smoked fish and dill, or slivers of rare roast beef can be mixed with a mustard flavoured mayonnaise.

Put the pasta on to cook. Make the mayonnaise by placing the egg yolk with the mustard and vinegar in the food processor. With the motor running, pour the oil in a drop at a time. When you have added about 2 tablespoons, increase the rate to a thin stream and add the rest of the oil (this should take about 4 minutes).

Once you have a thick mayonnaise add the dill, chop it into the sauce, and then thin with a little cream. Taste for seasoning, adding salt and pepper if necessary.

Meanwhile drain the pasta, run cold water through it and allow to cool.

Flake the cooked fish, removing bones as necessary. Toss the cooled pasta in the mayonnaise and carefully fold in the fish. Pile into a serving dish and sprinkle over the chopped onions.

Serve with an undressed watercress and tomato salad.

STRAWBERRIES IN CHAMPAGNE

**450 g/1 lb strawberries, washed and
    hulled**
¼ bottle champagne or sparkling wine
caster sugar
**a little brandy, or orange flavoured
    liqueur (optional)**

Slice the strawberries and divide them
between four glass dishes. Sprinkle over
a little sugar and a dash of brandy or
liqueur, if used. Allow the strawberries
to macerate in this until just before
serving, and then pour a little
champagne into each glass.

Menu 4

Lemon risotto

Sauté of spring vegetables

Papaya fans
with gingernut cream

serves 4

Lemon risotto

310 g/11 oz arborio or risotto rice
60 g/2 oz butter
2 tablespoons/olive oil
1 medium onion, finely chopped
6 tablespoons white wine
1 litre/2 pints boiling water, with 2
  vegetable stock cubes added
rind and juice of 1 large lemon
60 g/2 oz freshly grated Parmesan
  cheese
salt, pepper

I first tasted this wonderful lemon risotto at Badia in Chianti, the home of Lorenza de' Medici. I was looking in on one of the cooking classes she holds in this most beautiful Tuscan villa and this was the dish being taught. Lorenza explained that in her circle risotto could be served at even the most elegant of dinners, unlike pasta or polenta, as the arborio rice needed to make the perfect risotto was grown in only one small region of Italy, and thus was both rare and expensive.

Melt half the butter with the oil in a large heavy saucepan and cook the onion until transparent. (While doing this prepare the vegetables for the accompanying sauté, opposite.) Add the rice and stir, so it becomes coated with the oil/onion mixture. Pour in the wine and stir until it has been absorbed by the rice. Then, a ladleful at a time, add the boiling stock, stirring all the time. Keep adding the stock until the rice is bite-tender, but with a little resistance in the centre. Add the remaining butter, the lemon rind and juice and the cheese. Mix well and taste to check the seasoning, adding salt and pepper as necessary. Cover and leave to stand for at least 5 minutes.

SAUTÉ OF SPRING VEGETABLES

**450 g/1 lb mixed vegetables, e.g.
  broccoli, mangetout, courgettes, petit
  pois, baby corn, green beans**
2–3 spring onions
1 clove garlic
2 tablespoons good olive oil
salt, pepper

*Choose a selection of small fresh
vegetables for the sauté, with the
possible addition of some frozen petit
pois. Three or four different types will
give a good contrast of shapes and
colours.*

Prepare the vegetables and chop the
larger ones into approximately 5 cm/2
inch pieces. Slice the spring onions into
5 cm/2 inch sticks, peel and crush the
garlic. Heat the oil in a frying pan and
put in the onion and garlic. Fry for
about 1 minute to season the oil, and
then add the remaining vegetables. Stir-
fry for 4–5 minutes, until crisp-tender.
Season lightly.

   Pour the rested risotto into a large
serving dish and arrange the vegetables
in the centre. Extra lemon wedges can
be served alongside.

PAPAYA FANS
with gingernut cream

2 large ripe papayas
4 gingernut biscuits
150 ml/¼ pint double cream

Peel the papaya and slice in half
lengthways. Place the cut sides on a
board and cut slices from top to
bottom, starting about 1 cm/½ inch
below the apex of the fruit. Fan the
fruit out on to a serving dish.

   Roughly break the biscuits, and place
in a food processor with the cream.
Process for 1–2 minutes. Spoon next to
the fruit fans.

MENU 5

FRESH HERB RISOTTO

WILD & CULTIVATED MUSHROOM SAUTÉ

ICE CREAM MILLE FEUILLE

serves 4

FRESH HERB RISOTTO

285 g/10 oz risotto rice (arborio)
60 g/2 oz butter
2 tablespoons olive oil
900 ml/1½ pints light stock
1 medium onion, chopped
1 glass white wine (optional)
1 handful finely chopped fresh herbs,
** such as mint, rosemary, sage**
60 g/2 oz freshly grated Parmesan
** cheese**

When talking about probably the most Italian of dishes it is best to take advice from the experts. Antonio Carluccio is one of the most delightful and generous of men and has always been eager to share his love and knowledge of his native Italian food with the world. He serves wonderful risottos in the Neal Street Restaurant, in London's Covent Garden, made with any number of exotic ingredients, but this recipe – adapted from his beautiful book An Invitation to Italian Cooking *– is within reach of us all, and calls for nothing more complex than fresh garden herbs, rice, butter and cheese.*

Melt half the butter with the olive oil in a large pan. Bring the stock to the boil. Cook the onion in the hot fat until transparent, then add the rice and toss until it is well coated with the butter, oil and onion mixture. Add the white wine if using, and boil until reduced. Add 1 ladle of stock at a time and cook, stirring the risotto, until it is almost bite tender. Stir in the herbs and then add the remaining butter and the cheese. Beat lightly with a wooden spoon, cover and leave to rest for 5 minutes before serving.

Wild & cultivated mushroom sauté

340 g/12 oz mixed mushrooms (cleaned weight)
2 tablespoons olive oil
1 plump clove garlic, crushed
1 tablespoon chopped parsley
salt, pepper
fresh lemon juice to taste

As a reminder of Antonio's famed love of mushrooms I serve the risotto with a selection of sautéed mushrooms, both cultivated and wild, as the seasons allow.

Chop or tear the mushrooms into medium sized pieces. Heat the oil in a sauté pan, toss the mushrooms in the hot oil and cook, stirring, for 2–3 minutes. Add the garlic and stir well, cooking for a further 2–4 minutes. Season the mushrooms with parsley, salt, freshly ground black pepper and lemon juice to taste.

Ice cream mille feuille

2 ready-rolled sheets frozen puff pastry
a little milk to glaze
caster sugar
ice cream (bought or homemade, p. 150)

Preheat the oven to 220°C/425°F/Gas 7. Slice each sheet of pastry into four equal parts and place the eight pieces on a baking sheet. Brush four pieces of pastry, for the tops, with milk and sprinkle generously with sugar.

Bake the pastry for 10–12 minutes, until puffy and golden brown. Allow to cool. Sandwich the mille feuilles together with an ice cream of your choice just before serving.

Menu 6

Spanish rice
with spicy sausage

Green salad

Mocha mousse

Fresh cream

serves 4

Spanish rice
with spicy sausage

2 tablespoons olive oil
1 green pepper, chopped
1 red pepper, chopped
1 medium onion, chopped
2 fat cloves garlic, chopped
340 g/12 oz long-grain rice
1 × 400 g/14 oz tin chopped tomatoes in
  juice
600 ml/1 pint light stock
225 g/8 oz chopped chorizo sausage, or
  kabanos, or smoked ham
salt, pepper
1–2 tablespoons chopped fresh
  coriander

Heat the oil in a saucepan, stir in the
vegetables until well coated, and fry for
2–3 minutes. Add the rice and toss well
in the oil. Tip in the tomatoes and stir
well. Add the stock and bring to the
boil. Simmer the rice, partially covered,
until most of the water has been
absorbed.

Stir in the sausage, continue to cook
the rice until no liquid is visible and the
meat is heated through, and check the
rice for seasoning and bite. Add salt and
pepper to taste. Turn into a serving dish
and top with the fresh coriander.

Serve with fresh green salad.

Mocha mousse

170 g/6 oz plain chocolate
3 large eggs
1 tablespoon concentrated coffee and
  chicory essence (Camp)
cream, to serve

Separate the eggs, putting the whites
into a large, spotlessly clean bowl. Melt
the chocolate in a bowl, either over hot
water or in the microwave. Mix the egg
yolks and the coffee essence into the
chocolate, stirring well. Whisk the egg
whites until stiff but not dry and fold
into the chocolate mixture. Pour into
four serving glasses and chill until
needed.

Serve with cream.

Menu 7

Baked Pasta
with tomato, ham & black olives

Mincemeat & Hazelnut-Stuffed Apples

serves 4

Baked Pasta
with tomato, ham & black olives

450 g/1 lb quick-cooking pasta shapes
1 tablespoon olive oil
1 large onion, chopped
2 cloves garlic, crushed
1 jar passata (sieved tomatoes)
85 g/3 oz stoned black olives
½ teaspoon dried oregano
salt and black pepper
2 ham steaks, about 225 g/8 oz each
85 g/3 oz mozzarella cheese, sliced

Baked pasta dishes are very heartening on a cold day, but all too often they take hours of preparation and cooking. Here you can cheat by using quick-cooking pasta shapes that boil while a simple sauce simmers on the stove. Combine the two and bake in a hot oven for 15 minutes.

Put the pasta on to cook in a large pan of boiling salted water. In a frying pan heat the oil and slowly fry the onion with the garlic.

Heat the passata in a saucepan with the olives and herbs. Cut the ham steaks into 2.5 cm/1 inch cubes and simmer in the passata and herb mix for 5 minutes.

Drain the cooked pasta, and mix in the contents of the other two pans. Taste and adjust seasoning and pour into an ovenproof dish. Lay the cheese on top and bake in a hot oven, 200°C/400°F/Gas 6, for 15 minutes.

Mincemeat & Hazelnut-Stuffed Apples

4 large Golden Delicious apples
4 tablespoons mincemeat
30 g/1 oz hazelnuts, roughly chopped
30 g/1 oz butter
30 g/1 oz soft brown sugar
150 ml/¼ pint water

The apples bake alongside the pasta but take a little longer to cook, so will be ready in time for dessert.

Core the apples and cut a shallow line around the equator of each apple. Place them in a baking dish. Mix the mincemeat with the nuts and stuff the apples with this. Dot each apple with a knob of butter. Mix the sugar into the water and pour around the fruit. Bake in the oven, at 200°C/400°F/Gas 6, alongside the pasta, or after you have taken it out, for 20–25 minutes, basting once.

Menu 8

Vegetarian rice pilaf

Cucumber raita

Ice cream
with chocolate mallow sauce

serves 4

Vegetarian rice pilaf

2 tablespoons butter
1 medium onion, chopped
1 clove garlic, chopped
5 whole cardamom pods
1 × 10 cm/4 inch cinnamon stick
2 teaspoons ground cumin
1 teaspoon ground turmeric
¼ teaspoon cayenne pepper
300 g/10 oz long-grain rice
900 ml/1½ pints hot vegetable stock
450 g/1 lb mixed vegetables, such as
**   cauliflower, carrots, peas, beans**
salt, pepper
30 g/1 oz slivered almonds

This spiced rice dish can be made with a variety of vegetables. If you use leftover cooked vegetables, add them at the end of the cooking time and allow them to heat through.

Melt half the butter in a deep saucepan and fry the onion and garlic until beginning to brown. Add the whole spices and toss, then add the ground spices and stir-fry for 60 seconds. Put in the rice, give everything a good stir and then add the vegetable stock. Bring to the boil and simmer for 10 minutes. Add the prepared vegetables and continue to cook the rice until bite tender, adding a little more stock if necessary. Season to taste.

Fry the almonds in the remaining butter, and when golden scatter over the finished rice dish.

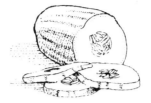

CUCUMBER RAITA

300 ml/½ pint thick natural yoghurt
½ cucumber, chopped into 1 cm/½ inch
  cubes
1 teaspoon ground coriander

Beat the yoghurt until smooth. Stir in
the cucumber and pour into a serving
dish. Sprinkle on the coriander.

ICE CREAM
with chocolate mallow sauce

1 block or tub ice cream (bought or
  homemade, p. 150)
6 marshmallows
115 g/4 oz plain chocolate
1 tablespoon butter
3 tablespoons hot water
slivered almonds

*I always keep a good variety of ice
creams in the freezer, both homemade
and the wonderful New England variety
available in good delicatessens. Each
person can choose a flavour and top it
with the hot sauce.*

With scissors snip the marshmallows
into small pieces. Melt the chocolate
with the butter over just simmering
water. When liquid, stir in the hot
water one tablespoon at a time; don't
worry if the mixture separates to start
with, just keep stirring. Keep the
mixture warm over the water with the
heat turned off, until needed. Just
before serving, mix in the snipped
marshmallows and a few slivered
almonds, then pour over the ice cream.

MENU 9

SAFFRON RICE
with fish

TINNED RED PEPPER SALAD

BAKED BANANAS

FRESH CREAM OR ICE CREAM

serves 4

SAFFRON RICE
with fish

30 g/1 oz butter
1 medium onion, chopped
a pinch of saffron threads
1 glass dry white wine
285 g/10 oz long-grain rice
600 ml/1 pint light stock
225 g/8 oz monkfish, cod or haddock
  (skinned weight)
salt and pepper
1 tablespoon chopped fresh chervil or
  parsley

This lightly scented rice dish can stretch a small amount of fish to feed four. Saffron gives out most taste and flavour if lightly toasted before being crushed with a pestle or the back of a spoon.

Melt the butter in a saucepan and fry the onion until transparent.

In the bowl of a long-handled kitchen spoon toast the saffron over a gas flame. This will take a few seconds. Crush the strands to a powder and dissolve in the wine. Reserve. Put the rice into the onion mixture and stir well. Add the saffron and wine, stir and then add the stock. Mix well, cover and simmer for 10–12 minutes.

Push the fish pieces gently into the rice and continue to cook for a further 5 minutes, or until the rice is tender and the fish just cooked, adding a little more hot stock if necessary. Season to taste with salt and freshly ground black pepper, and top with herbs.

Tinned red pepper salad

1 × 400 g/14 oz tin red peppers
  (pimentos)
2 tablespoons extra virgin olive oil
freshly ground black pepper
fresh basil, parsley or chervil torn into
  small pieces

*Tinned pimentos can be transformed by
careful rinsing to remove the brine, and
by dressing with virgin olive oil.*

Drain the tinned peppers and rinse
carefully under running water. Pat dry
with kitchen paper and slice into strips.
Arrange on a serving dish, pour on the
oil, add a little black pepper and
sprinkle over the fresh herbs.

Baked bananas

4–6 bananas, depending on size
60 g/2 oz butter
60 g/2 oz light muscavado sugar
1 teaspoon cinnamon
½ teaspoon ground ginger
1 tablespoon rum, or orange juice

Slice the bananas into an ovenproof
dish. Melt the butter in a saucepan, stir
in the remaining ingredients and pour
over the fruit. Cover the dish with foil
and bake in a preheated oven, at
180°C/360°F/Gas 4, for 15–20 minutes.
  Serve warm with cream or ice cream.

Menu 10

Pan-fried pork fillet
with cider & fresh pears

New potatoes

Buttered spinach

Jam soufflé omelette

serves 4

Pan-fried pork fillet
with cider & fresh pears

4 × 12 cm/5 inch pieces of pork fillet,
  ready trimmed by the butcher
1½ tablespoons olive oil
1 large shallot, chopped
150 ml/¼ pint dry cider
150 ml/¼ pint light stock
2 large firm dessert pears, peeled and
  quartered
1 teaspoon redcurrant jelly
salt and pepper to taste
1 teaspoon arrowroot, slaked with
  1 tablespoon water (optional)

*Pork fillet is a quick-cooking dream.
Tender, moist and delicious, it has a
light flavour that readily adapts to any
number of sauces. I particularly like
cooking pork with cider as they do in
northern France, where cider is the
regional drink. I like fresh pears, so I
have used these rather than the more
traditional apples. Serve this with new
potatoes or plain boiled rice, and
spinach (see p. 109).*

Put the potatoes or rice on to cook.

In a heavy frying pan heat the oil and
brown the pork fillet on all sides.
Remove from the pan and keep warm.
Add the shallot to the pan juices, stir
and fry until golden brown. Pour in the
cider to deglaze the pan, scraping up
any brown bits that have stuck to the
bottom. Replace the pork, pour over
the stock and add the pears. Simmer for
6–7 minutes.

Remove the pork and pears from the
pan, slice the pork into medallions and
arrange with the pears on a heated
serving dish. Turn up the heat and boil
the sauce to reduce by one-third. Stir in
the redcurrant jelly, and season to taste.
If liked, thicken the sauce with the
slaked arrowroot. Pour this over the
pork and serve with spinach and
potatoes or rice.

JAM SOUFFLÉ OMELETTE

3 large eggs, separated
3 tablespoons caster sugar
1 tablespoon butter
3–4 tablespoons warm raspberry jam

Jam soufflé omelettes went out of fashion when families could no longer afford to hire cooks. But they are delicious, and if you are eating supper in the kitchen they make a wonderful and unusual finale to a meal.

Using an electric whisk, beat the egg yolks with the sugar until pale and light. In a separate bowl whisk the whites until stiff; this can be done by hand in 2–3 minutes. Heat a 20 cm/8 inch frying pan over a moderate heat and melt the butter in it. Fold the yolks and egg whites together and pour the mixture into the pan. Cook over a low heat for 5–6 minutes without stirring.

Have the grill hot and slip the omelette pan underneath it. Cook the top of the omelette until puffy and golden. Mark a fold line down the centre of the omelette, and pour on the warm jam.

Turn the omelette over and out on to a serving dish. Sprinkle with extra caster sugar if desired and serve at once.

Menu 11

Chicken Skewers
with spicy sauce

Hot French Bread

Mixed Salad
with walnut oil dressing

Fresh Pears
with Parmesan cheese

serves 4

Chicken Skewers
with spicy sauce

575 g/1¼ lb boneless, skinless chicken
   meat
1 clove garlic
1 medium onion
150 ml/¼ pint fresh orange juice
2 tablespoons soy sauce
1 teaspoon sesame oil
1 dry red chilli, crushed
1 tablespoon black treacle
freshly ground black pepper

for the sauce
150 ml/¼ pint chicken stock
1 teaspoon arrowroot (optional)

I use ready-boned chicken thighs and breasts to make these chicken skewers. If you have time, put them into the marinade in the morning. Hot French bread goes well with these kebabs to mop up the sauce and clean the plate before eating the salad.

Put all the ingredients except the chicken and stock in a blender or processor and whizz until the onion and garlic are chopped and the marinade is smooth. Cut the chicken into cubes roughly 2 cm/1½ inches square and place them in the marinade. Refrigerate until needed.

When you are ready to cook the chicken, thread the chunks loosely on to skewers and grill under a preheated grill for 10–15 minutes, turning often. Meanwhile, put the marinade ingredients into a saucepan along with the chicken stock and boil for 5 minutes. If the sauce is not sufficiently reduced, thicken with a little slaked arrowroot.

Serve the skewers with a little sauce spooned over them and hand the rest separately.

MIXED SALAD
with walnut oil dressing

a selection of small salad leaves
fresh large leaf herbs e.g. chervil,
coriander, flat leaf parsley, basil
1 tablespoon chopped walnuts
2 tablespoons walnut oil
salt and freshly ground black pepper
1–2 teaspoons white wine vinegar

*Serve this salad after the spicy chicken
to give a contrast with the rich sauce.
Use as many different salad leaves as
you can find. Fresh herbs can be mixed
in with endive, radiccio, rocket and
lamb's lettuce. There is no need to chop
the large herb leaves – just add them
whole to give a salad that looks as
varied as it tastes.*

Mix the salad leaves and herbs in a
large serving bowl. Add the nuts, the
oil, a little salt and pepper and 1
teaspoon of vinegar. Toss together well
and taste the dressing. If necessary, add
a little more vinegar or seasoning.

FRESH PEARS
with Parmesan cheese

4 large ripe dessert pears
1 teaspoon lemon juice
115–170 g/4–6 oz piece Parmesan cheese

If time allows peel the pears, slice them
and arrange each on a dessert plate.
Brush the cut surfaces with a little
lemon. Using a sharp knife or a cheese
slicer, chip or cut the Parmesan into
large flakes, and divide these among the
dishes. Serve immediately.

MENU 12

PAN-FRIED FILLET OF LAMB
with ginger & mint

BASMATI RICE

GREEN BEANS
with garlic

AMARETTI ICE CREAM
SANDWICHES
with raspberry sauce

serves 4

PAN-FRIED FILLET OF LAMB
with ginger & mint

725 g/1½ lb lamb fillet, trimmed
1 tablespoon oil
1 shallot, chopped
1 teaspoon powdered ginger
2 tablespoons dry sherry
150 ml/¼ pint lamb or vegetable stock
1 tablespoon redcurrant jelly
salt and pepper
1 tablespoon chopped fresh mint

Lamb fillet is rather fattier than pork but it has a wonderfully sweet taste and is very tender. Ask the butcher to trim it as best he can and then fry it over a high heat to crisp the remaining fat. Serve the lamb with basmati rice.

Put the basmati rice on to boil.

Heat the oil in a large frying pan and fry the fillets, whole, until brown on all sides but still pink in the centre (about 6 minutes). Remove from the pan and keep warm. Fry the shallot in the oil, and when translucent add the ginger and stir-fry for 60 seconds. Deglaze the pan with sherry and allow to cook down. Add the stock and the redcurrant jelly and simmer, stirring occasionally, for 3–5 minutes. Taste and adjust the seasoning if necessary before stirring in the mint.

Carve the lamb into pieces, stir any juices into the sauce and then spoon it over the lamb.

Green beans
with garlic

**450 g/1 lb green beans, topped and
tailed
60 g/2 oz butter
1 large plump clove garlic, sliced
salt and freshly ground black pepper**

These beans take about 7 minutes to
cook.

Place the beans in a large pan and
cover with boiling water. Boil over a
high heat until just cooked, 3–4
minutes. Drain and reserve. Melt the
butter in the pan and add the garlic. Fry
in the hot fat for a few minutes before
adding the beans. Toss the beans in the
garlic butter and season well with
pepper and salt. When the beans are
sizzling hot, serve with the lamb and
rice.

Amaretti ice cream
SANDWICHES
with raspberry sauce

**285 g/10 oz frozen raspberries, thawed
icing sugar to taste
squeeze of lemon juice
2 Amaretti biscuits per person (4 halves)
block or tub ice cream (bought or
homemade, p. 150)**

*A very quick dessert can be made using
exotic biscuits as the wafers in these ice
cream sandwiches.*

Make the sauce when you start to cook.
In a food processor purée the fruit with
sugar and lemon juice to taste. Sieve
and reserve.

If the ice cream is not one of the soft
varieties, move it from the freezer to the
fridge when you sit down to eat so it
softens slightly.

When you are ready to serve,
sandwich each biscuit together with a
generous spoonful of ice cream and
arrange on a plate. Serve with raspberry
sauce.

MENU 13

TWICE-GRILLED FISH
with lemon chive sauce

NEW POTATOES

BROCCOLI

REFRIGERATOR CHOCOLATE SLICE

serves 4

TWICE-GRILLED FISH
with lemon chive sauce

4 fish fillets
30 g/1 oz butter
30 g/1 oz flour
300 ml/½ pint creamy milk
salt and pepper
grated rind and juice of half a lemon
2 tablespoons chopped chives
60 g/2 oz freshly grated Parmesan

Simply grilled fish fillets or thawed fish portions are napped with a lemon and chive sauce, scattered with freshy grated Parmesan cheese and grilled again.

Arrange the fish fillets in a well greased ovenproof dish and cook under a preheated grill, turning once until the flesh flakes when the tip of a knife is inserted (5–7 minutes).

Meanwhile make the sauce. Melt the butter in a saucepan, add the flour and stir together. Gradually beat in the milk and simmer for 2–3 minutes. Season to taste with salt and pepper and then stir in the lemon rind, juice and the chives.

Take the dish from under the grill and carefully pour the sauce over the fillets. Sprinkle the cheese evenly over the fillets and return to the grill. Grill until the cheese is golden brown.

Serve with potatoes and broccoli.

REFRIGERATOR CHOCOLATE SLICE

8 large digestive biscuits
30 g/1 oz glacé cherries, chopped
30 g/1 oz slivered almonds
1 tablespoon brandy, or fresh orange juice
60 g/2 oz plain chocolate
30 g/1 oz soft butter

Make the chocolate slice as far in advance as possible to allow it to set.

Roughly crush the biscuits and mix in the cherries and nuts. Pour over the brandy or juice and stir well. Melt the chocolate and stir in the butter. Pour this over the biscuit mixture and stir until well combined. Pour the mixture into a shallow cake tin and press down. Place in the fridge.

When ready, cut into small slices and serve.

MENU 14

ASPARAGUS, EGGS, JERSEY POTATOES & HAM

FRENCH APPLE TART

FRESH CREAM

serves 4

ASPARAGUS, EGGS, JERSEY POTATOES & HAM

per person
115 g/4 oz asparagus (trimmed weight)
1–2 large free-range eggs
115 g/4 oz baby Jersey Royal potatoes
85 g/3 oz York ham, or similar
butter
salt, black pepper

This is one of my favourite spring meals. It provides a wonderful contrast of tastes and textures: tender green asparagus, earthy Jersey Royal potatoes, the freshest free-range eggs, salty York ham and lashings of creamy butter. Because you are relying on the natural taste of the ingredients, buy the best you can find.

Bring two large pans of water to the boil. Place the eggs in a third pan and cover with cold water. Start cooking the potatoes first – they will take 18–20 minutes. The asparagus will take about 10 minutes and the eggs about 7 minutes.
   Arrange the sliced ham around the edge of a huge serving dish and pile the vegetables and eggs in the centre.
   Serve each person with ham, potatoes and asparagus. Everyone then takes an egg to peel and mash with lots of butter, salt and freshly ground black pepper to make a sauce.

FRENCH APPLE TART

1 × 225 g/8 oz pack frozen puff pastry, thawed
4 Golden Delicious apples
sugar

My apple tart is simplicity itself. Serve it hot from the oven with very thick cream. This whole meal is rather indulgent, but there is always tomorrow to nibble a lettuce leaf.

Preheat the oven to 220°C/425°F/Gas 7.
   Roll the pastry out thinly and place on a baking sheet. Peel, core and slice the apples and arrange them on the pastry, pressing them in slightly. Sprinkle with sugar and allow to sit for 10 minutes. Bake in the preheated oven for 20 minutes, or until the pastry is puffed and golden and the sugar on the apples has melted.
   Serve with cream.

MENU 15

CHEESE SOUFFLÉS
with salsa

BAKED APPLE SLICES
with muesli & soured cream

serves 4

CHEESE SOUFFLÉS
with salsa

45 g/1½ oz butter
45 g/1½ oz flour
300 ml/½ pint milk
85 g/3 oz Cheddar cheese, grated
salt and pepper
nutmeg
1 tablespoon dry breadcrumbs, mixed
with 1 teaspoon dry mixed herbs
4 eggs, separated

for the salsa
2 large tomatoes
3 spring onions, chopped
1 clove garlic, chopped, to taste
1 fresh chilli, chopped, or a dash of
Tabasco
juice of 1 lime
fresh coriander, chopped
½ teaspoon wine vinegar
sugar to taste
salt and pepper

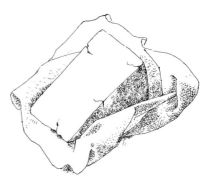

You'll have to work quickly to make this meal in 30 minutes, but it's such a good supper that I want to include it here.

Start with the sauce for the soufflés and then prepare the salsa and apples while the soufflés cook. If you don't have individual dishes, improvise using deep soup bowls – just so long as they are ovenproof.

Preheat the oven to 200°C/400°F/Gas 6.

Start with the sauce. Melt the butter in a saucepan, stir in the flour and then add the milk a little at a time. Stir in the cheese and season very well with salt, pepper and grated nutmeg. Simmer the sauce for 2 minutes. Allow to cool for 2 minutes while you prepare the dishes.

Oil four individual soufflé dishes about 10 cm/4 inches in diameter, coat the inside with the crumb/herb mixture, and put to one side. Whip the egg whites until stiff but not dry.

BAKED APPLE SLICES
with muesli and soured cream

4 large Golden Delicious apples
1 tablespoon soft butter
1 tablespoon soft brown sugar
1 tablespoon fresh orange juice
4 tablespoons crunchy muesli
soured cream to serve

Now beat the yolks one at a time into the cheese sauce, then fold in the whites gently but thoroughly. Divide between the dishes and bake for 15–20 minutes until well risen and golden brown on top. The soufflés should be soft in the middle.

While the soufflés are baking, prepare the salsa. Put the tomatoes in a bowl and cover with boiling water for 60 seconds to loosen the skins. Peel and chop the tomatoes, and mix with the onions, garlic and chilli. Stir in the remaining ingredients.

This sauce can be made in a food processor, but the texture may be a little too uniform.

When the soufflés are cooked, take them to the table and open the centre with a spoon. Spoon a little of the salsa into each dish and pass the rest separately. Take care as the dishes will be very hot.

Golden Delicious make very good cooking apples as they don't fall apart, but of course you may use a homegrown variety if you wish.

Put the pudding in to cook when you take out the soufflés.

Mix together the butter and sugar and spread in a 20 cm/8 inch ovenproof dish. Cut the apples into quarters and remove the core. Slice each quarter into three and arrange these in the dish. Pour over the juice and scatter on the muesli. Bake in the oven, turning the heat down to 180°C/360°F/Gas 4, for 10–15 minutes or until needed. Serve with soured cream.

Menu 16

Chicken
in cheese sauce

Rice

Mangetout peas

Mississippi mud pie

serves 4

Chicken
in cheese sauce

4 boneless chicken breasts
1 tablespoon olive oil
1 shallot, finely chopped
salt and black pepper
30 g/1 oz butter
30 g/1 oz flour
450 ml/¾ pint creamy milk
115 g/4 oz mature Cheddar cheese,
  grated
½ teaspoon Dijon mustard
½ teaspoon sweet paprika

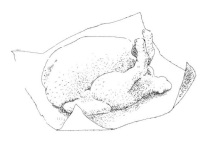

Chicken breast fillets are delicious and easy to eat but they can be overcooked and dry out if you're not careful. I pan-fry the fillets while I'm making the sauce and then finish them in a hot oven.

Serve this with rice and mangetout peas.

Preheat the oven to 190°C/380°F/Gas 5.

Heat the oil in a frying pan and cook the shallot for 1 minute. Season the chicken breasts and cook in the pan over a medium heat, turning once while you make the sauce.

Melt the butter in a saucepan, stir in the flour and gradually incorporate the milk to make a sauce. Simmer the sauce for 2 minutes, stirring, then add the mustard, paprika, salt, pepper and three-quarters of the cheese. Put the chicken in an ovenproof dish, pour over the sauce and sprinkle on the remaining cheese. Bake uncovered for 15 minutes, or until needed.

Mississippi mud pie

200 g/7 oz chocolate digestive biscuits
60 g/2 oz butter, melted
600 ml/1 pint chocolate ice cream
   (bought or homemade, p. 151)
60 g/2 oz plain chocolate chips, or
   crumbled chocolate flake bar

*Make the crust of the pie first and put
into the coldest part of your freezer.
Unless you are using 'soft scoop', put
the ice cream into the fridge to soften as
you sit down to eat. The pie takes
moments to assemble just before
serving.*

In a food processor, whizz the biscuits
to make crumbs, then pour in the
melted butter and mix for a further few
seconds. Tip the mixture into a loose-
bottomed flan tin and press down
evenly over the base and sides. Put into
the freezer.
   When you are ready to serve, spoon
the softened ice cream into the pie shell
and then place the shell on a serving
plate. Scatter on the chocolate chips or
flakes and serve at once. Any leftover
pie can be kept in the freezer until
needed.

Menu 17

Scallop & salmon ceviche

Hot herb bread

Fresh apricot & nectarine turnovers

Cream or fromage frais

serves 4

Scallop & salmon ceviche

340 g/12 oz cleaned scallops (white muscle only)
340 g/12 oz skinned and boned salmon
2 red onions, finely sliced
juice of 4 limes
juice of 2 lemons
1 small dried chilli, crushed
ground black pepper and salt
1 tablespoon chopped fresh parsley

to serve
2 ripe avocados
lettuce leaves

When serving fish that is 'cooked' only by the action of the marinade, do make sure that it is absolutely fresh. Ask the fishmonger to skin and bone a tail joint of salmon for you and if you can, buy a few of the scallop shells. They make delightful serving dishes for a variety of fish and seafood.

Wash the fish and pat dry. Slice the scallops as thinly as possible into medallions. Cut the salmon into 1.5 cm/ ¾ inch dice. Arrange the fish in a deepish serving dish and scatter over the onion rings.

Mix the remaining ingredients together and pour this marinade over the fish. Toss gently to make sure everything is coated in the mixture, and then cover and place in the fridge until needed.

When ready to serve, stone and slice the avocados and arrange half a fruit in a fan on each of four plates. Add the lettuce leaves. Divide the fish between the leaves and spoon any remaining marinade on top.

Serve with Hot herb bread, below.

Hot herb bread

1 French stick
fresh parsley and tarragon
1 clove garlic, finely chopped
115 g/4 oz butter, softened

Chop the herbs and garlic into the butter. This may be done in a food processor. Cut the loaf lengthways through the middle, stopping at the bottom crust, and then crossways at 2.5 cm/1 inch intervals, again stopping at the bottom crust. Spread the butter on the cut sides of the bread, wrap the loaf in foil and bake in a hot oven, at 190°C/380°F/Gas 5, for 10 minutes. Open the foil and bake for a further 5 minutes.

Fresh apricot & nectarine turnovers

2 squares ready-rolled puff pastry,
** thawed**
2 ripe nectarines
3 ripe apricots
½ teaspoon ground cinnamon
30 g/1 oz sugar
30 g/1 oz butter
1 tablespoon flaked almonds

to finish
milk, to glaze
sugar, for sprinkling

Old-fashioned though fruit turnovers may be, the idea of baking fruit wrapped in pastry and so keeping in every drop of juice is an excellent one. When fresh apricots and nectarines aren't available use tinned fruit sharpened with a little lemon juice or brandy.

Cut each sheet of pastry in half. Slice the fruit, discarding the stones, and divide them between the pastry rectangles. Mix the cinnamon with the sugar and sprinkle over. Dot with butter and almonds.

Dampen the edges of one half of the rectangle and turn over the other half, forming a square. Press the edges with the prongs of a fork to seal. Place the turnovers on a baking sheet and brush with milk, then sprinkle liberally with sugar. Allow them to sit until you take the herb bread from the oven. Turn the heat up to 220°C/425°F/Gas 7, and cook for 15–20 minutes, until puffed up and golden.

Serve with cream or fromage frais.

Menu 18

Pan-fried breast of grouse
with wild mushrooms & fresh pasta

Carrot sticks

Greek yoghurt
with toasted almonds & clear honey

serves 4

Pan-fried breast of grouse
with wild mushrooms & fresh pasta

breast fillets of 4 grouse
salt and pepper
4 tablespoons red wine
olive oil
20 button onions, peeled and left whole,
  or 1 large onion, finely chopped
1 plump clove garlic, crushed
butter
4 slices of white bread
225 g/8 oz fresh tagliatelle
60 g/2 oz dried porcini mushrooms,
  soaked in 150 ml/¼ pint warm water
2 tablespoons brandy
300 ml/½ pint jellied stock

While it may seem extravagant to use only the breast of these expensive game birds, in reality it is often only the breasts that are worth eating. If time permits, save the rest of the carcass to make good stock for this dish. Stock cubes won't do, so if you can't use homemade, choose commercially prepared fresh stock from the chilled food counter of the supermarket.

Serve with lightly boiled carrot sticks.

Season the grouse breasts with pepper and put into the wine mixed with 1 tablespoon olive oil to marinate until needed. Glaze the onions by frying gently with the garlic in 2 tablespoons olive oil and 1 tablespoon butter, remove to a serving dish and keep warm. Cut the crusts from the bread and cut each slice in half, then fry these in the hot fat to make 8 croûtes. Drain on absorbent paper and keep warm.

Put the pasta on to boil, drain when *al dente*, toss in a little butter and keep warm.

Pat the grouse breasts dry and fry them in the hot oil/butter mixture, adding more if needed, for 3–4 minutes each side, then keep warm. Drain the mushrooms and fry in the oil, then add the brandy. Allow this to bubble, stir well, then pour in the stock. Boil rapidly for 2–3 minutes to reduce to a concentrated sauce.

To serve, place each breast on a croûte and, allowing two per person, arrange on plates with some onions and a little sauce. Hand the remaining sauce and the pasta separately.

GREEK YOGHURT
with toasted almonds & clear honey

**450 g/1 lb strained Greek cows milk
  yoghurt
85 g/3 oz slivered almonds
wildflower honey**

*This is a very simple dessert, and ideal
after the robust flavours of the grouse.
If possible use Greek honey from
Mount Hymettus. This delicious mixed-
flower honey can be found in speciality
food shops.*

Toast the almonds by dry-frying them
over medium heat in a non-stick frying
pan. Toss the almonds about to ensure
they are evenly cooked, then allow to
cool.
  Divide the yoghurt between four
dessert bowls and drizzle over a
spoonful of honey, then top with the
almonds.

MENU 19

GAMMON STEAKS
with orange mustard sauce

HERB-BAKED CHERRY TOMATOES

MASHED POTATOES

MICROWAVE POACHED PLUMS

FRESH CREAM

serves 4

*Note: begin by cooking the tomatoes
and potatoes.*

GAMMON STEAKS
with orange mustard sauce

**4 gammon steaks
2 tablespoons wholegrain mustard
about 6 tablespoons fresh orange juice
2 egg yolks
85 g/3 oz soft butter, cut into small
   cubes
salt, pepper**

*This is a really easy meal to prepare.
Use a thick bottomed pan over
moderate heat and beat the sauce
constantly with a balloon whisk. The
mustard flour has a stabilizing effect on
the eggs. Thin the completed sauce to
taste with a little extra juice.*

Heat the grill, and about 10 minutes
before serving, cook the gammon steaks
for 4–5 minutes each side, turning as
necessary.

Make the sauce. In a heavy pan, mix
the mustard with 4 tablespoons fresh
orange juice. Heat until the mixture
boils. Remove from the heat and
gradually add the egg yolks, beating
constantly to thicken the sauce. Add the
butter cubes all at once, still beating.
When the sauce is smooth, taste to
check the seasoning, adding 1–2
tablespoons more juice if desired.

Serve with mashed potatoes and
cherry tomatoes (opposite).

HERB-BAKED CHERRY TOMATOES

450 g/1 lb cherry tomatoes
2 tablespoons olive oil
a few sprigs fresh thyme or tarragon
salt and black pepper

Cherry tomatoes make an excellent hot vegetable baked with fresh herbs and a little olive oil. Being sweet, and very juicy, they are especially suitable with grilled food.

Put the washed tomatoes into an ovenproof dish and drizzle on the oil. Tear up the herbs and sprinkle these over the tomatoes. Season with salt and freshly ground black pepper and bake in a preheated oven, at 180°C/360°F/ Gas 4, for 30 minutes.

MASHED POTATOES

725 g/1½ lb peeled potatoes, such as
** King Edward**
salt and pepper
butter

Cut the potatoes into 5 cm/2 inch chunks. Put them in a deep saucepan, cover with cold water and bring to the boil before you start the gammon. Simmer them until soft, about 15–20 minutes. Drain and mash well, using plenty of butter and seasoning.

MICROWAVE POACHED PLUMS

725 g/1½ lb large ripe plums
sugar

Fruit cooked in the microwave has an intensity of flavour that is hard to beat. Little or no water is needed and the fruit cooks in minutes. Do check your manufacturer's instructions if in doubt about how to use your oven.

Wash the plums and cut each one in half, leaving in the stones. Place the cut fruit in a wide microwave-proof bowl and add 2–3 tablespoons sugar. Leave to sit for 10 minutes to allow the juices to run.

When you are ready to cook the plums, cover with suitable film or an upturned plate, and microwave for 5 minutes on high, stirring once. Allow the plums to rest for 2 minutes, check for sweetness, and add more sugar if necessary.

Serve warm with cream.

MENU 20

SPANISH TORTILLA

SALAD

HOT BREAD
with olive butter

APPLES & CHEESE

serves 4

SPANISH TORTILLA

1 large Spanish onion, sliced
3–4 medium potatoes, peeled and cut
   into 1 cm/½ inch cubes
1 red or green pepper, chopped
1 large clove garlic, chopped
2–3 tablespoons olive oil
6 large eggs, beaten with salt and
   pepper

A tortilla is a Spanish omelette, a completely different type of omelette to the more usual fluffy one. Instead of being cooked quickly over a hot flame, the tortilla is slowly cooked, without stirring, and sometimes finished under the grill.

Though a traditional tortilla contains only onion, potato and garlic, besides eggs, I add beans, peas or other leftover vegetables if I have them around.

Heat the oil in a large, preferably non-stick frying pan. Put in the sliced onion and potatoes and cook for 10 minutes over a medium heat. Add the peppers and garlic and fry for a further 3–4 minutes. Pour over the beaten eggs and move the vegetables around in the pan to form an even layer. Continue to cook the omelette over a low heat, without stirring, for 10–15 minutes, or until the eggs are set. If the centre is still runny when the base is cooked brown, heat the grill and put the frying pan under it for 2–3 minutes to cook the top.

Turn out on to a plate and serve, cut into wedges, with salad, hot bread and Olive butter, below.

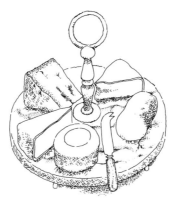

Olive butter

115 g/4 oz soft butter
85 g/3 oz stoned black olives
pepper

Making seasoned butters is a quick way to liven up a simple meal. Here I have used olives, but you could try a whole range of flavours, including Stilton, herbs, anchovy and tuna.

In a food processor, chop the olives into the butter. Season with a little black pepper. Scrape out into a dish and refrigerate until needed.

Serve with hot bread.

Apples & cheese

You may think I'm cheating by suggesting apples and cheese as a dessert. But what could be more delicious than a ripe apple and an equally ripe piece of English cheese?

I also want to draw attention to the exciting new 'old' apples that are coming back on to the market. Now, I like Golden Delicious apples on occasions, they cook well and the newer blushed variety has a better flavour. But nothing can beat Old English apples, and at last we can again, at the right time of year, find such treats as Tydemans Early Worcesters, Jonagold or Lord Lambourne.

The flavour of cheese is so often spoilt by refrigeration. Sadly, in today's kitchen a north-facing pantry with a marble shelf is a rarity, so buy cheese as you need it, store well wrapped in greaseproof paper – not cling film – and let it come to room temperature before you eat it.

MENU 21

STIR-FRIED CHICKEN
in lemon chilli sauce

RICE

STIR-FRIED BROCCOLI
with fresh ginger juice

CHOCOLATE SHELLS FILLED
with chestnut cream

serves 4

STIR-FRIED CHICKEN
in lemon chilli sauce

4 boneless chicken breasts
juice of 1 large lemon
2 tablespoon peanut oil
4–6 spring onions, chopped
1 green chilli, deseeded and sliced
2 carrots, cut into sticks
1 tablespoon dry sherry, or rice wine
2 tablespoons light soy sauce
200 ml/⅓ pint chicken stock
1 tablespoon lemon marmalade
2 teaspoons arrowroot, slaked with 2
**   tablespoons water**

I searched and searched for the right combinations to make this chicken dish. I was looking for a sauce that was both hot and sharp, but with undertones of sweetness. Just when I thought I wouldn't quite be able to match the taste on my plate to the idea in my head, I tried adding a spoonful of lemon marmalade – and there it was.

Slice the washed chicken and put into the lemon juice to marinate.

Heat the oil in a wok or large pan and fry the spring onion and chilli. Add the chicken and stir-fry for 2 minutes, then add the carrots. Stir-fry for a further 2 minutes, then add the sherry, soy sauce and stock. Bring to the boil and simmer, stirring occasionally, for 4 minutes. Stir in the marmalade, and as soon as it has dissolved, the slaked arrowroot. Continue to cook to thicken the sauce and taste to check seasoning. Add extra soy if needed.

Serve with rice and Stir-fried broccoli (opposite).

STIR-FRIED BROCCOLI
with fresh ginger juice

450 g/1 lb broccoli florets
2 tablespoons peanut oil
1 teaspoon sesame oil
salt
2.5 cm/1 inch cube fresh ginger root
4 tablespoons water
1 tablespoon sesame seeds

Heat the two oils together in a large frying pan and stir-fry the broccoli, seasoning with a little salt. Put the ginger in a garlic press and squeeze the juice over the broccoli. Add the water. Stir in the sesame seeds and continue to stir-fry until the broccoli is cooked crisp-tender and the liquid has evaporated.

CHOCOLATE SHELLS FILLED
with chestnut cream

4 ready-made chocolate dessert shells
either: 1 small tin sweetened chestnut
**   purée,**
or: 225 g/8 oz natural chestnut purée,
**   and 60 g/2 oz icing sugar, sifted, and**
**   ½ teaspoon vanilla essence**
1 tablespoon brandy
300 ml/½ pint whipping cream
chocolate leaves to decorate

Ready-made chocolate shells can be bought from most supermarkets or speciality food stores and are a whizz to have at hand. Almost anything looks good in the elegant moulds and this chestnut brandy cream is superb. This is an excellent festive sweet, perfect for a Christmas meal.

If you are using unsweetened chestnut purée, begin by beating the icing sugar and vanilla into it. It will start out rather dry, but softens in moments. Add the brandy to the purée. Whip the cream until quite firm and then fold in the sweetened purée.

Arrange the chocolate shells on individual plates and divide the cream between them. Decorate with chocolate leaves.

MENU 22

GRILLED SWORDFISH
with tomatoes & pesto

PASTA & STEAMED COURGETTES

STRAWBERRIES
with rose-scented cream

serves 4

GRILLED SWORDFISH
with tomatoes & pesto

4 swordfish steaks (or fresh tuna)
4 tablespoons olive oil
4 tablespoons lemon juice
1 clove garlic, chopped
salt and pepper
2 large ripe tomatoes
4 tablespoons pesto

I first tasted swordfish and fresh tuna when holidaying on Long Island. We ate the tuna fresh from the sea, cut into thick steaks and grilled on the barbecue, and I was amazed how good it was served with herb butter and the sweetest cobs of white corn. Swordfish is more delicate and overcooks quickly, so take great care when you grill it. Use either fish in this recipe. Serve pesto with the fish and a side dish of pasta and some steamed courgettes.

Wipe the fish and put into a shallow dish. Mix the oil, lemon, garlic and pepper together and pour over the fish. Leave to marinate as long as possible. If you have time, do this in the morning, if not, 10 minutes will suffice.

Put the tomatoes in a bowl and cover with boiling water for 60 seconds, remove the skins and chop the flesh.

Heat the grill and cook the fish for about 4 minutes each side, turning once and basting. To check the fish is cooked, insert the point of a knife in the flesh: it should be opaque.

When the fish is cooked, serve topped with a spoonful of pesto and a spoonful of chopped tomato, and a bowl of noodles and courgettes (opposite).

PASTA & STEAMED COURGETTES

340 g/12 oz fresh ribbon noodles
450 g/1 lb young courgettes
salt and pepper
virgin olive oil

Bring a large pan of water to the boil. If you have a steamer that fits on this pan so much the better, otherwise you will need two pans of boiling water.

Cut the stalks from the courgettes and slice into sticks, sprinkle with salt and put into the steamer. When you are ready to cook the pasta – 3–6 minutes before serving – put it into the boiling water and put the courgettes, in the steamer, on top. Cook until the pasta is *al dente* and the courgettes still have a little bite. Drain the pasta and tip into a warm serving dish. Pour on 2 tablespoons virgin olive oil and toss. Arrange the courgettes on top. Season with freshly ground black pepper and serve.

STRAWBERRIES
with rose-scented cream

450 g/1 lb strawberries
4 tablespoons dessert wine (optional)
300 ml/½ pint whipping cream
1–2 tablespoons caster sugar
½ teaspoon triple strength rosewater
rose petals to decorate

Wash, hull and slice the strawberries. Divide them between four dessert bowls. If you have a bottle of dessert wine open, pour 1 tablespoon over each portion. Whip the cream until it begins to thicken, then add the sugar and rosewater, and continue beating until the cream is thick. Spoon the cream over the berries and top with one or two pale pink rose petals.

MENU 23

BULGAR
with chickpeas & walnuts

CHERRY TOMATO &
MOZZARELLA SALAD

FRESH PEACHES
with raspberry coulis & fromage frais

serves 4

BULGAR
with chickpeas & walnuts

340 g/12 oz bulgar
900 ml/1½ pints water
1 red pepper
2 medium sized red onions
1 plump clove garlic
1 handful fresh parsley
1 handful fresh coriander
4–5 tablespoons olive oil
juice of half a lemon
1 teaspoon wine vinegar
salt, pepper
1 × 400 g/14 oz can chickpeas, drained
60 g/2 oz walnut kernels, chopped

Bulgar is a nutty nutritious grain that is soaked in water and then mixed with a mass of different seasonings. I like lots of chopped red onion, lemon juice and fresh coriander, and whatever else takes my fancy. To give balance to this vegetarian meal I have included some chickpeas and walnuts for extra protein.

Put the bulgar to soak in the water for 30 minutes. Deseed and chop the pepper, chop the onions, crush the garlic and chop the herbs. When the bulgar has soaked, drain it well, pressing out any excess water. Mix in the oil, lemon juice, and vinegar and season with salt and black pepper. Toss in the remaining ingredients and taste to check the seasoning. If necessary add extra lemon juice, oil, salt or pepper.

Cherry tomato & mozzarella salad

450 g/1 lb cherry tomatoes
1 packet mozzarella cheese, preferably
   mozzarella di bufala
1–2 tablespoons virgin olive oil
salt and black pepper
fresh basil leaves

Drain the cheese and cut into 2 cm/³/₄ inch squares. Mix the cheese with the tomatoes and pour over the oil. Season to taste and top with a few basil leaves, roughly torn into large pieces.

Fresh peaches
with raspberry coulis & fromage frais

4 large ripe peaches
225 g/8 oz raspberries (thawed if frozen)
1 tablespoon icing sugar
1 teaspoon lemon juice
190 g/7 oz 8% fromage frais

Fresh peaches are made more elegant if they are skinned before serving. Simply place them in a bowl of boiling water for 1–2 minutes, and the skins will slip off easily.

Put the peaches in a bowl and cover with boiling water. After 2 minutes, slip off the skins, slice each peach in half and reserve.

Rub the raspberries through a sieve or Mouli and beat the sugar and lemon juice into the purée.

Beat the fromage frais. Place a spoonful of fromage frais on each plate, arrange two peach halves on top and carefully spoon the sauce around. Decorate with mint leaves. Hand the remaining fromage frais separately.

Menu 24

Lettuce soup

Pitta toasts

Chef's salad
with creamy avocado dressing

serves 4

Lettuce soup

1 tablespoon vegetable oil
1 medium onion, finely chopped
225 g/8 oz lettuce leaves, shredded
1 medium potato, diced
600 ml/1 pint chicken stock
2–4 tablespoons cream

Fortunately, not all summer soups have to be served cold. I like the idea of a soup that can be served hot or cold, depending on the warmth of the evening, and lettuce soup fits the bill, thriftily using the outside leaves of the salad needed below.

Heat the oil in a saucepan and fry the onion for 2–3 minutes. Stir in the lettuce and potato and cook for 1 minute. Pour in the stock and bring to the boil. Simmer the soup for 6–10 minutes and then liquidize in a food processor or blender.

Bring back to the boil, remove from the heat and stir in the cream. Serve at once with hot pitta bread.

Chef's salad

lettuce leaves
170 g/6 oz sliced ham, cut into strips
170 g/6 oz sliced turkey, cut into strips
170 g/6 oz mature Gouda cheese, cut into strips
4 plump spring onions, sliced
2 large (or 4 medium) ripe tomatoes, quartered
½ cucumber, peeled and sliced

for the creamy avocado dressing
1 ripe avocado
150 ml/¼ pint soured cream
2 tablespoons lemon juice
1 clove garlic
1 tablespoon chopped parsley
salt and freshly ground black pepper

Chef's salad is a wonderful catch-all for any amount of different ingredients, but there are a few basics: good lettuce to line the dish, at least two different meats, a waxy cheese such as Gouda, large ripe tomatoes, sweet onions and a distinctive dressing.

For the dressing, remove the avocado from its skin and discard the stone. Put all the ingredients into a blender or processor and mix until smooth. Taste and correct the seasoning.

Line four bowls with the lettuce leaves, arrange the salad ingredients inside, and pour over a little dressing. Hand the remainder separately.

Menu 25

Mushroom consommé

Lamb chops
with lemon honey mint butter

New potatoes

Peas

serves 4

Mushroom consommé

900 ml/1½ pints concentrated chicken or beef stock
115 g/4 oz open mushrooms, finely sliced
1 small glass dry sherry (optional)
1 small green chilli, deseeded and sliced

Make this soup with either homemade stock or a good quality ready-made stock, and use open mushrooms for maximum flavour. I sometimes add a very finely sliced green chilli to the soup, which is how it was served to me in Mexico.

Simmer the stock in a saucepan for 5 minutes with the mushrooms and chilli if using. Add the sherry, taste and correct the seasoning.

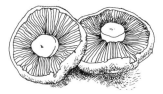

Lamb chops
with lemon honey mint butter

8 lamb chops, trimmed and seasoned with salt and pepper
85 g/3 oz butter
1 teaspoon honey
2 tablespoons chopped mint
grated rind of half a lemon

Simply grilled lamb chops can be made special with savoury butter. Serve with new potatoes and peas.

First make the butter: in a bowl beat the softened butter with the honey, mint, lemon rind, and seasoning. Take a piece of foil and spoon on the butter, shaping it into a log. Wrap the foil around the log and place in the freezer until needed.

Heat the grill and cook the chops for 5–8 minutes each side, while you eat the soup.

To serve: unwrap the butter log and place a slice on each chop.

MENU 26

EGGS
with Mediterranean vegetables

CRUSTY BREAD

CHOCOLATE SURPRISE PUDDINGS
serves 4

EGGS
with Mediterranean vegetables

1–2 tablespoons olive oil
1 large onion, sliced
2 cloves garlic, crushed
1 medium aubergine
225 g/8 oz courgettes
1 tin chopped tomatoes
½ teaspoon herbes de Provence
salt, pepper
8 size 3 eggs
4 tablespoons grated Gouda cheese

*Don't worry about sweating the
aubergine with salt if it is a young fresh
one. Fresh vegetables have much more
crunch, but you could use ready-made
ratatouille if you wish, and bake the
eggs in a medium oven for
8–10 minutes. Serve with crusty bread.*

In a large frying pan heat the oil and fry
the onion and garlic. Cut the aubergine
into 2.5 cm/1 inch cubes and slice the
courgettes. Add them to the pan and fry
for 2–3 minutes, then add the tomatoes,
herbs, salt and pepper. Stir well and
simmer for 10 minutes. Heat the grill.

Mix the ratatouille, taste and correct
the seasoning. Make 8 depressions in
the surface of the ratatouille and
carefully break an egg into each one.
Cover the pan with a lid and cook for 2
minutes. Remove the lid, sprinkle on
the cheese and brown under the
preheated grill for 2–3 minutes.

CHOCOLATE SURPRISE PUDDINGS

115 g/4 oz soft margarine
115 g/4 oz caster sugar
2 size 2 eggs, beaten
115 g/4 oz self-raising flour
30 g/1 oz cocoa powder

for the sauce
generous 300 ml/½ pint hot water
85 g/3 oz soft brown sugar
2 heaped tablespoons cocoa powder

In a food processor whizz the margarine
with the sugar until light, add the eggs
one at a time and process until well
combined. Sift in the flour and cocoa
and mix in using short bursts of power.
Don't overprocess at this stage.

Divide the mixture between four
greased ovenproof dishes. Mix the
sauce ingredients together in a jug and
pour the mixture over the puddings.
Don't worry if it all looks a little
strange.

Bake the puddings in a preheated
oven, at 190°C/380°F/Gas 5 for 25–30
minutes. Serve with cream.

MENU 27

GRATIN OF CARROT & PARSNIPS

TROPICAL TRIFLES

serves 4

GRATIN OF CARROT & PARSNIPS

450 g/1 lb carrots, peeled
450 g/1 lb parsnips, peeled
45 g/1½ oz butter
2 shallots, chopped
1 clove garlic, crushed
salt and black pepper
300 ml/½ pint double cream
60 g/2 oz freshly grated Parmesan
cheese

This gratin is a wonderful dish to make if you have a mixture of meat- and non-meat-eaters at the same table. Delicious on its own, the gratin can also be served as an accompaniment to grilled chicken, steak or chops.

Have a large pan of salted water boiling. Preheat the oven to 190°C/380°F/Gas 5.

Cut the carrots and parsnips into matchsticks. I use the chip attachment on my food processor, which does this in seconds. Put them into the water and boil for 5 minutes, drain and reserve.

In a large cast iron gratin dish, melt the butter, fry the shallots for 2 minutes and then add the garlic. Switch off the heat and put in the carrots and parsnips. Toss the vegetables in the butter/onion mixture and season well with salt and black pepper. Pour over the cream and sprinkle the cheese evenly over the top.

Bake in the oven for 15–20 minutes until bubbling hot and the cheese is brown. Serve with warm granary rolls.

TROPICAL TRIFLES

225 g/8 oz stale light fruit cake or trifle
sponges
30 g/1 oz flaked almonds
2 ripe bananas, sliced
115 g/4 oz fresh or tinned pineapple,
chopped
1–2 tablespoons dark rum
ginger marmalade
300 ml/½ pint ready-made custard

I've used a time-saving ready-made custard for these trifles: for choice, buy a chill-fresh custard with a real cream base.

In a large bowl mix the cake, crumbled into smallish pieces, the nuts, fruit and rum. Toss well together and divide between four ramekins. Top each with a teaspoon of ginger marmalade and some custard. Decorate with a few extra almonds if desired. Refrigerate until needed.

MENU 28

EGGS BAKED IN MUSHROOM
CAPS
with tarragon cream

CRUSTY BREAD

GREEN SALAD

LITTLE FRUIT CHARLOTTES

serves 4

EGGS BAKED IN MUSHROOM
CAPS
with tarragon cream

8 medium sized open mushrooms
1 shallot, chopped
1 tablespoon butter
oil
salt and freshly ground black pepper
8 size 3 free-range eggs
several sprigs fresh tarragon
150 ml/¼ pint double cream

Once I had tried baking eggs in open mushrooms I couldn't think why I hadn't done it before. The mushrooms make the perfect foil for the richness of the eggs and cream, and tarragon is the perfect herb to complement both.

Take the stems from the mushrooms, chop them and fry them with the shallot in the butter. Grease a baking dish big enough to take the mushrooms in a single layer. Heat the oven to 200°C/400°F/Gas 6.

Wipe the mushroom caps, brush the outsides with oil and arrange in the dish. Divide the shallot mixture between the caps and season well with salt and black pepper. Break an egg into each cap and place a few tarragon leaves on top. Run 1 spoonful of cream over each egg and then bake for 10–15 minutes in the oven.

Serve with crusty bread and a green salad.

Little Fruit Charlottes

**1 tin apricot halves, drained, or 6 fresh
  apricots, halved
115 g/4 oz blackberries
170 g/6 oz granary bread
60 g/2 oz butter
60 g/2 oz soft brown sugar**

*Fruit charlottes can be made with
almost any fruit. Apricots and
blackberries make a colourful, tangy
mixture.*

Grease four ramekin dishes and divide
the fruit between them. In a food
processor, whizz the bread into crumbs.
Melt the butter with the sugar and stir
in the crumbs. Divide this mixture over
the fruit and bake in a preheated oven,
at 190°C/380°F/Gas 5, for 15 minutes.

MENU 29

VEGETABLES IN LEMON SAFFRON
SAUCE
with sesame puff pastry fingers

RHUBARB
with honey & rosewater

FROMAGE FRAIS OR THICK
CREAM

serves 4

VEGETABLES IN LEMON SAFFRON
SAUCE
with sesame puff pastry fingers

1 sheet ready-rolled puff pastry, thawed
beaten egg, to glaze
sesame seeds, for sprinkling
1 kg/2 lb prepared assorted baby
    vegetables, such as corn, asparagus
    tips, carrots, sugar snap peas, French
    beans
1 pinch saffron
150 ml/¼ pint warm milk
300 ml/½ pint single cream
30 g/1 oz butter
30 g/1 oz plain flour
rind and juice of 1 large lemon
salt and pepper

If you haven't time to allow a pie filling to cool before covering with pastry, simply bake the pastry separately, cut into fingers, and serve on top of the filling. For this recipe you will need a selection of baby vegetables and two microwave cook-bags. Alternatively, boil the vegetables briefly in the normal way. Buying prepared vegetables is a real timesaver, and now at least one high street store sells them packed in a bag that can be popped straight into the microwave oven.

Heat the oven to 220°C/425°F/Gas 7.

Cut the pastry sheet into fingers 5 cm/2 inches wide and 10 cm/4 inches long and brush these with beaten egg or milk. Sprinkle them generously with sesame seeds and bake until well risen and golden brown, about 10 minutes.

Divide the vegetables between the two cook-bags, putting one tablespoon of water into each one. Seal loosely with the plastic tags provided.

Toast the saffron in a large kitchen spoon over a hot plate or gas flame for

RHUBARB
with honey & rosewater

**675 g/1½ lb rhubarb
honey to sweeten
1–2 tablespoons triple strength
rosewater**

a few seconds until it darkens in colour. Tip on to a plate and crush with the back of the spoon. Sprinkle this powder over the warm milk.

Make the sauce by melting the butter in a saucepan, stirring in the flour and gradually beating in the cream. Allow the sauce to simmer while you beat in the saffron flavoured milk, then the lemon juice and rind. Season to taste with salt and freshly ground black pepper.

Put the vegetables into the microwave oven and cook for 7 minutes on high, moving them at least once during the cooking time. Allow to rest for 2 minutes.

Warm a serving dish. Drain the vegetables by piercing a hole in each bag and allowing any water to run out, then arrange the vegetables in the dish. Pour over the hot sauce and top with the sesame fingers.

Once the vegetables are cooked you can use the microwave to prepare this rose-scented rhubarb sweetened with honey. If you can get it, buy the rhubarb variety called Champagne.

Cut the washed rhubarb into pieces and place in a dish suitable for use in a microwave oven. Cover loosely with film and cook for 4–5 minutes, turning once. Remove from the oven, stir in the honey and rosewater and leave to rest for 1 minute. Taste to check the flavouring and adjust as necessary. Note: if the rhubarb is very mature, it may need longer cooking.

Serve with fromage frais or thick cream.

MENU 30

WATERCRESS SOUP

PAN-FRIED PORK
with prunes

STEAMED CARROTS & COURGETTES

serves 4

WATERCRESS SOUP

450 g/1 lb floury potatoes
1 small onion, chopped
1 teaspoon oil
1 litre/2 pints chicken stock
170 g/6 oz watercress
salt and pepper
150 ml/¼ pint single cream

If you have any pure white soup bowls use them to serve this beautifully green soup.

In a large saucepan fry the onion in the oil for 2 minutes. Peel and chop the potatoes into 2.5 cm/1 inch dice. Add these to the pan, stir and then pour in the stock. Add half the watercress, roughly chopped, and a little salt and pepper. Bring to the boil and simmer for 10 minutes.

Pour the soup into a blender and process until smooth. Tip all but one third back into the pan. Put the remaining watercress into the blender with the remaining soup and blend until finely chopped. Stir this into the soup in the pan and reheat. Add the cream, taste, adjust the seasoning and serve.

PAN-FRIED PORK
with prunes

4 × 12.5 cm/5 inch pieces trimmed pork
  fillet
2 tablespoons olive oil
salt and pepper
1 shallot, chopped
1 clove garlic
2 tablespoons armagnac or brandy
150 ml/¼ pint concentrated stock
8 plump 'ready-to-eat' prunes
1 tablespoon soft butter

Pork with plump Agen prunes is a traditional dish from the southwest of France. Fry the pork in large pieces and carve just before serving to give moist, tender medallions.

Steamed carrots & courgettes

285 g/10 oz carrots
285 g/10 oz courgettes
butter
salt and pepper

Heat the oil in a large frying pan and fry the seasoned pork, turning, until brown all over and cooked through (7–10 minutes). Remove to a serving dish and keep warm.

Fry the shallot and garlic in the remaining fat, and when transparent, deglaze the pan with the brandy. Stir everything well, scraping any bits that have stuck to the pan.

Pour in the stock, add the prunes and simmer until the sauce has reduced and thickened slightly. Stir in the butter to give a gloss to the sauce.

Slice the cooked pork and serve with the sauce. I like to serve carrot and courgette sticks with this rich dish.

Peel the carrots and slice them and the courgettes into matchsticks. Have a pan of boiling water ready and put the carrot sticks to steam. After 5 minutes, add the courgettes and continue to steam until the vegetables are cooked to your liking. Toss with a little butter, salt and black pepper and serve.

MENU 31

TUNA BEIGNETS

AVOCADO, ONION & TOMATO
SALAD
with chilli and lime salsa

OAT & PLUM CRUMBLES

FROMAGE FRAIS OR CREAM

serves 4

Note: rub the fat into the flour for the crumble in your food processor before making the choux to save having to wash it between uses.

TUNA BEIGNETS

60 g/2 oz butter
150 ml/¼ pint water
75 g/2½ oz plain flour
½ teaspoon salt
2 size 3 eggs, beaten
170 g/6 oz flaked tuna
30 g/1 oz freshly grated Parmesan cheese
1 teaspoon Dijon mustard
½ teaspoon paprika
freshly ground black pepper
oil for frying

to serve
Parmesan, paprika, black pepper

These delicious deep-fried spoonfuls of choux pastry make a tasty supper dish, but they can also be served as a starter course or, made teaspoon-sized, as a canapé.

Beignets can be made with tuna as in this recipe, but you could also try salmon, smoked haddock, chopped prawns or a robust Cheddar, Stilton or Roquefort.

Serve the beignets with a sharp salad salsa to offset their richness.

Make the dough. Melt the butter in the water in a medium sized non-stick saucepan. Bring to the boil and add the flour all at once. Turn off the heat. You can put the mixture into a food processor at this stage. Beat until smooth. Allow to cool for 2–3 minutes. Beat in the eggs one at a time; the mixture should be stiff and glossy. Now beat in the remaining ingredients.

If using a processor, use short bursts of power and don't over-process.

When you are ready to cook the beignets, heat about 2.5 cm/1 inch of oil in a large pan and fry dessertspoons of the mixture a few at a time, turning once, until they are golden brown and puffed (3–4 minutes). Continue until all the mixture is used, keeping the cooked beignets warm. Serve at once, sprinkled with a mixture of Parmesan, paprika and pepper, and accompanied by the salad salsa (opposite).

Note that these beignets freeze very well and can be reheated in a medium oven for 10 minutes.

Avocado, onion & tomato salad
with chilli and lime salsa

2 large ripe tomatoes
1 medium red onion
2 ripe avocados
juice of 1 lime
1 small green chilli, seeded and sliced
1 teaspoon wine vinegar
1 clove garlic, crushed
¼ teaspoon sugar
salt and pepper

Skin the tomatoes by covering with boiling water for 60 seconds. Slice the onion finely, remove the avocado from its skin, discard the stone and slice; slice the tomatoes. Arrange the prepared salad on a platter. Mix the remaining ingredients together for the dressing and pour over.

Oat & plum crumbles

450 g/1 lb plums
85 g/3 oz butter
115 g/4 oz plain flour
60 g/2 oz oats
60 g/2 oz soft brown sugar

In a food processor, rub the fat into the flour, then mix in the oats and sugar. Grease four ramekins, slice and divide the plums between them. Spoon on the topping and bake the crumbles in a preheated oven, at 190°C/380°F/Gas 5, for 15–20 minutes.

Serve with fromage frais or cream.

MENU 32

GAZPACHO

GOATS CHEESE SALAD
with fresh figs & grilled peppers

FRESH CRUSTY BREAD

serves 4

GAZPACHO

1 large red onion
1 plump clove garlic
½ cucumber
½ green pepper deseeded
2 thick slices white bread
2 tablespoons warm water
3 tablespoons virgin olive oil
1–2 tablespoons wine vinegar
1 litre/2 pints good tomato juice
salt, pepper

I keep cartons of tomato juice in the fridge ready to make this lovely Spanish summer soup. Use a food processor to grate the vegetables and prepare the breadcrumbs.

First grate the onion, garlic, cucumber and green pepper in the food processor. Empty these into a large bowl and put this in the fridge. In the food processor (there is no need to rinse it) using the metal knife, process the bread and water. Add the oil and vinegar and process again. Tip this into the bowl of grated vegetables.

Mix in the tomato juice and season with salt and pepper. Add 1 tray of ice cubes, stir and allow to sit in the fridge until needed.

GOATS CHEESE SALAD
with fresh figs & grilled peppers

1 large red pepper
assortment of baby salad leaves
4 large or 8 small ripe fresh figs
340 g/12 oz goats cheese
virgin olive oil
wine vinegar
salt and black pepper

Slice the pepper into quarters and remove the seeds. Heat the grill and put the pepper, skin side up, close to the element. Cook until the skin is black. Remove from the pan and cover with a damp cloth.

Arrange the salad leaves on a plate. Peel and slice the figs and arrange these on the plate. Slice the cheese and place on the salad.

Uncover the peppers and peel off the skins. Slice into strips and arrange over the cheese. Drizzle a tablespoon of oil over each salad and add a few drops of vinegar. Season to taste.

Serve with fresh crusty bread.

MENU 33

BAKED FRESH TUNA
with garlic & sun-dried tomatoes

BOILED POTATOES

GREEN SALAD

BREAD, BUTTER & MARMALADE
PUDDINGS

serves 4

BAKED FRESH TUNA
with garlic & sun-dried tomatoes

4 tuna steaks
3 tablespoons olive oil
juice of 1 lemon
salt and pepper
1 clove garlic, thinly sliced
6 sun-dried tomatoes, chopped
1 tablespoon chopped chives

Fresh tuna can be dry if overcooked, so I like to bake it wrapped in paper or foil, with some robust seasonings. Serve this dish with some plain boiled potatoes and, to freshen the palate, a green salad as a separate course.

Mix the oil, lemon juice and freshly ground pepper, and put the steaks in it to marinate for at least 10 minutes. Take four pieces of foil about 30 cm/12 inches square and place a piece of fish on each one with some of the marinade. Divide the garlic, tomatoes and chives between the fish fillets and wrap the foil around to make four loose parcels.

Bake in the oven, at 180°C/360°F/Gas 4, for 15–20 minutes, checking the tuna is cooked by inserting the tip of a knife into one fillet to see if the centre of the fish is opaque.

BREAD, BUTTER & MARMALADE
PUDDINGS

225 g/8 oz fruit bread
60 g/2 oz butter
2 tablespoons orange marmalade
2 size 3 eggs
60 g/2 oz caster sugar
1 tablespoon orange brandy (optional)
300 ml/½ pint single cream

The all-time nursery favourite, bread-and-butter pudding, can be made even more special by spreading a little marmalade on to the bread. For an even more indulgent pudding, add a little orange brandy to the cream and egg custard.

Grease four ramekin dishes. Slice the bread and spread with butter and marmalade. Divide the bread between the dishes, making some of the points stick up out of the dish. Beat the eggs, sugar and brandy with the cream and strain over the bread. Allow to sit for 10 minutes, then bake in the oven alongside or after the fish, at 180°C/360°F/Gas 4, for 25–30 minutes.

Menu 34

Blackened fish fillets

Lemon rice

Fried courgettes in cream

Eton mess

serves 4

Note: start by making the dessert and cooking the rice.

Blackened fish fillets

**4 fillets of cod, skinned and boned
  (thawed frozen fillets are ideal)
3 tablespoons Creole seasoning (p. 174)
1 tablespoon oil**

Creole spice (p. 174) is a wonderfully pungent mixture that brightens up even the plainest fish fillets. Here the simply grilled fish is balanced with courgettes in cream sauce and tangy lemon scented rice.

Sprinkle the fillets on both sides with spice. Reserve. When you are ready to cook, heat the grill and put the fillets on the grill pan. Drizzle the oil over the fillets and grill until the fish is cooked through, turning once (about 10 minutes).
   While the fish is grilling, cook the courgettes.

Lemon rice

**1 shallot, chopped
1 tablespoon butter
225 g/8 oz long-grain rice
rind and juice of 1 lemon
salt and pepper
600 ml/1 pint water**

Fry the shallot in the butter until soft, stir in the rice, lemon rind and juice. Season with salt and pepper and add the water. Bring to the boil, half-cover the pan and simmer until the rice is cooked and the water absorbed.

FRIED COURGETTES IN CREAM

340 g/12 oz young courgettes
30 g/1 oz butter
1 plump clove garlic, crushed
salt and black pepper
200 ml/⅓ pint double cream

Cut the courgettes into sticks. Melt the butter in a large non-stick frying pan. Stir-fry the courgettes for 2–3 minutes, add the garlic and cook for 1 minute. Season well with salt and lots of black pepper and pour in the cream. Simmer, stirring, for 2–3 minutes or until the cream is slightly reduced. Serve at once.

ETON MESS

450 g/1 lb fresh strawberries
4 individual meringue cases
300 ml/½ pint whipping cream

to finish
4 small strawberries
mint leaves

Eton mess provides one way of using up egg whites. The meringue cases can be made in advance (p. 153), or you can buy them boxed, in the supermarkets.

Wash and hull the strawberries. Slice them into a bowl and mash very lightly with a fork. Crumble the meringues. Beat the cream until fairly stiff but not solid. Fold the fruit and meringue into the cream and divide the mixture between four dessert glasses. Decorate with the small strawberries, and mint leaves.

CHAPTER
3

1-hour meals

THESE MENUS MAY take an hour, but the preparation time is usually quite fast: it's the cooking that takes 40 minutes or so.

Some of these delicious three-course meals make very elegant party food. I love the mussel pies, the chicken and almond soup and the tomato, mustard and cheese tart, but as I read through what's on offer, I find I want to make all the good things in this chapter again.

I have put some more adventurous recipes in here, but they are always combined with simpler ones to allow the cook as much freedom as possible.

Menu 1

Smoked fish pie

Carrot & courgette 'pasta'

Citrus & ginger compote

serves 4

Smoked fish pie

340 g/12 oz boned, skinned white fish
   such as haddock, monkfish, cod or
   whiting
340 g/12 oz smoked haddock or cod
400 ml/⅔ pint milk
bay leaf
peppercorns
30 g/1 oz butter
115 g/4 oz button mushrooms, sliced
juice of half a lemon

for the sauce
30 g/1 oz butter
30 g/1 oz flour
milk reserved from cooking fish
150 ml/¼ pint single cream
salt and pepper
1 tablespoon chopped chives
1 teaspoon grated lemon rind

for the topping
725 g/1½ lb potatoes, peeled
4–6 anchovy fillets
60 g/2 oz butter

*This pie is a family favourite, though
not featured on our menu as often as
my husband would like. When a friend
remarked that surely I cooked fish pie
for him, his reply was that I used to
before the recipe was just right, but
then I moved on! Mashing a few
anchovy fillets into the potato really
lifts this dish out of the schoolroom.*

Bring the potatoes for the topping to
the boil and cook until soft. Drain and
mash.

Poach the fish in the milk with the
bay leaf and a few peppercorns for 4–5
minutes, or until it is just cooked.
Remove, reserving the milk. Take any
skin and bone from the fish, and flake
the larger pieces.

Melt the butter in a pan and fry the
mushrooms for a few minutes. Add the
lemon juice, cook for a few minutes to
boil off the liquid, and add to the
prepared fish.

Make the sauce by melting the butter,
adding the flour to make a roux, and
then gradually beating in the strained
fish liquor and finally the cream. Season
to taste with black pepper and salt, then
stir in the chives and lemon rind. Fold
the fish and mushrooms into this
mixture and spoon into a deep
ovenproof dish.

For the topping, mash the anchovy
fillets with the back of a fork and then
mash them with the butter into the
cooked potato. Spoon this over the fish
and bake the pie in a preheated oven, at
190°C/380°F/Gas 5, for 30 minutes.

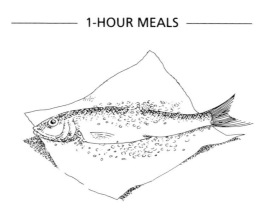

CARROT & COURGETTE 'PASTA'

4 medium carrots
4 medium courgettes
a knob of butter
salt and pepper

Carrot and courgette 'pasta' is a visual joke, where the vegetables are shaved into long slivers to resemble pasta ribbons.

With a potato peeler, peel the carrots and then continue to shave fine long strips of carrot. Shave the courgettes in the same manner, leaving on the green skin.

Steam the vegetables over boiling water for 5–7 minutes and then toss with butter and a little seasoning to serve.

CITRUS & GINGER COMPOTE

2 pink grapefruit
3 sweet oranges
2 pieces stem ginger, sliced into fine matchsticks
2 tablespoons sugar
150 ml/¼ pint water
2 tablespoons ginger syrup

With a sharp knife cut the peel and pith from the fruit and divide into segments. Put the fruit and any juice into a serving bowl along with the ginger.

Melt the sugar in a heavy bottomed pan and cook until lightly browned. Pour in the water and stir until the caramel has dissolved. Allow to cool, add the ginger syrup, and pour over the fruit.

Menu 2

Chicken & Almond Soup

Fresh Salmon Steaks in Filo

Beurre Blanc

Petits Pois

Pears in Red Wine

serves 4

Chicken & Almond Soup

1 litre/2 pints good chicken stock, either homemade or chill fresh
115 g/4 oz peeled whole almonds
salt, pepper
1 teaspoon chopped fresh chives

This wonderful soup has really only two ingredients, so they must be the very best; a full flavoured chicken stock and good sweet almonds. The finished soup is very concentrated and looks wonderful in fine white porcelain consommé dishes.

Skim as much fat from the cold stock as possible. Process the almonds in a food processor until finely chopped, add a little stock and process for a further 2 minutes. Tip this mixture into a saucepan with the remaining stock and simmer for 30 minutes. Season to taste with salt and pepper and serve hot with the chives sprinkled on top.

Fresh Salmon Steaks in Filo

4 boneless, skinless salmon fillets
1 packet filo pastry, thawed
2 tablespoons chopped dill
salt and pepper
150 ml/¼ pint soured cream
30g/1 oz butter, melted

Ask the fishmonger to skin and fillet the salmon for you or use prepared fillets from the supermarket. Work fast, keeping the filo covered with a damp cloth as it dries out quickly.

Have a damp cloth to cover the filo while you work.

Mix the dill and a little seasoning into the soured cream. Butter a sheet of filo and top with another sheet. Place the fish towards one end and place a quarter of the seasoned cream on top. Wrap the pastry round the fish like a parcel and seal all the edges with melted butter. Place each parcel on a baking sheet until needed, brushing the pastry with butter.

Heat the oven to 220°C/425°F/Gas 7, and bake for 20 minutes, or until golden. Serve with beurre blanc (opposite) and petits pois.

Beurre blanc

1 shallot, finely chopped
1 small glass white wine
2 tablespoons wine vinegar
1 tablespoon double cream
85 g/3 oz butter, diced
salt and pepper

Use a heavy saucepan and a balloon whisk.

Cook the shallot in the wine and vinegar until all but 2 tablespoons have evaporated. Add the cream, and as soon as it boils turn off the heat. Beating continuously, add the cubes of butter. Season to taste. Once the sauce is smooth, serve with the fish.

Pears in red wine

4 large, nearly ripe pears
300 ml/½ pint red wine
60 g/2 oz caster sugar
1 stick cinnamon

Peel the pears and lay them in a dish just big enough to take them. Mix the wine with the sugar and pour this over the pears. Put in the cinnamon stick and bake the pears in the oven for 30–40 minutes, or until tender. Allow to cool slightly and serve with cream.

Menu 3

Fricassee of Seafood
in chilli sauce with fennel

Fresh Pasta

Syrup & Ginger Tart

Cream or Ice Cream

serves 4

Fricassee of Seafood
in chilli sauce with fennel

1.5 kg/3 lb fresh mussels
450 g/1 lb monkfish (boned, skinned
  weight)
1 glass white wine
1 large onion, chopped
2 tablespoons olive oil
2 cloves garlic, crushed
1 large head fennel, chopped
1 green chilli, deseeded and chopped
400 g/14 oz tin tomatoes
30 g/1 oz sun-dried tomatoes
salt and pepper
lemon juice
fresh parsley or coriander, chopped

While in the north of Europe we serve fish with creamy white sauces, the Mediterranean countries have no such inhibitions, combining even delicately flavoured seafood with robust tomato-based sauces. Almost any combination of fish can be used, as long as the general quantities are kept the same. Serve with fresh pasta.

Scrub the mussels clean under cold water and discard any that are broken or do not close when tapped. Put the wine, a glass of water and a little chopped onion into a large saucepan and bring to the boil. Put in the mussels and cover the pan. Cook over a high heat for 2–3 minutes, stirring the mussels once or twice. Transfer the mussels to a wide dish and discard any that have not opened.

Syrup & ginger tart

340 g/12 oz shortcrust pastry
285 g/10 oz golden syrup
30 g/1 oz butter
285 g/10 oz fresh brown breadcrumbs
  (granary for preference)
lemon juice and grated rind
1–2 teaspoons powdered ginger

Allow the liquor to boil and reduce to 150 ml/¼ pint. Strain through a sieve lined with kitchen paper and reserve.

Meanwhile, fry the remaining onion in the oil in a large saucepan for about 2 minutes. Add the garlic and fennel, give them a good stir, and fry for another 2 minutes. Now add the chilli, both types of tomatoes and the strained mussel liquor. Stir well, season with pepper and simmer the sauce for 15 minutes until thick.

Cut the monkfish into 2.5 cm/1 inch cubes and press these down under the surface of the sauce. Simmer for about 5 minutes, or until the fish is just opaque.

While the sauce is cooking, remove the mussels from their shells. Stir them into the mixture to heat through. Add a squeeze of lemon juice, sprinkle with parsley or coriander and serve on fresh pasta.

Treacle tart is most often made with golden syrup, and I like to lift the rather cloying flavour with a little ginger and a squeeze of lemon.

Line a loose-bottomed flan tin with shortcrust pastry. Heat the syrup and butter together and stir in the crumbs, a squeeze of lemon juice and a little grated rind, and the ginger. Pour this mixture into the pastry case and level the top. Bake the tart in a preheated oven, at 180°C/360°F/Gas 4, for 45 minutes, or until golden.

Serve warm with cream or ice cream.

Menu 4

Little mussel pies

Steamed green beans

Warm chocolate brownie

Ice cream

serves 4

*Note: cook the Chocolate brownie
before the Mussel pies.*

Little mussel pies

1.5 kg/3 lb mussels
¼ bottle white wine
2–3 stalks parsley
5 or 6 black peppercorns
1 medium onion, chopped
15 g/½ oz butter
**170 g/6 oz oyster mushrooms, torn into
  pieces**
1 small glass fino sherry
2 tablespoons chopped chives
2 tablespoons chopped parsley
225 g/8 oz puff pastry
beaten egg for brushing

for the sauce
30 g/1 oz butter
white of 1 medium leek, chopped
30 g/1 oz flour
150 ml/¼ pint double cream
300 ml/½ pint strained mussel liquor
salt and pepper to taste

*Mussels are so much easier to prepare
these days as they are now available in
almost grit-free bags. Give them a good
scrub and discard any that are broken
or remain closed after they are cooked.*

*Serve the pies with steamed green
beans.*

To cook the mussels, bring the wine to
the boil in a large saucepan and add the
parsley, peppercorns and onion. Simmer
for 2 minutes. Put in the mussels and
boil vigorously, stirring occasionally,
until the mussels have opened, 3–5
minutes.

Remove the mussels, boil the liquor
to reduce to 300 ml/½ pint, strain and
reserve.

To make the sauce, melt the butter and lightly fry the leeks. Add the flour and make a white sauce using the cream and mussel liquor, then simmer for 2–3 minutes. Season to taste.

Meanwhile melt the remaining butter and fry the mushrooms for 2–3 minutes. Pour in the sherry and allow to bubble for 1 minute, stirring constantly. Pour this into the cream sauce. Add the chives and parsley.

The mussels should by now be cool enough to handle. Take them from their shells and divide them between four ovenproof dishes. Pour a quarter of the sauce into each dish.

Roll out the puff pastry and cut four circles large enough to cover your chosen dishes. Grease the edges of the dishes and cover with the pastry lids, pressing the sides on well. Cut a small vent for the steam to escape, brush with beaten egg and bake in a preheated oven, at 220°C/425°F/Gas 7, for 15–20 minutes.

Serve at once with steamed green beans.

Warm chocolate brownie

100 g/3½ oz plain flour
1 teaspoon baking powder
30 g/1 oz cocoa
¼ teaspoon salt
115 g/4 oz soft margarine
140 g/5 oz caster sugar
2 size 3 eggs
½ teaspoon vanilla essence
60 g/2 oz chopped walnuts, optional

Serving chocolate brownie still warm from the oven is another wonderful idea from the United States. It goes beautifully with ice cream.

Mix the flour, baking powder, cocoa and salt together. Cream the margarine with the sugar and then beat in the eggs one at a time, and the vanilla essence. Fold in the flour mixture and the walnuts, if using. Pour into a greased 17.5 cm/7 inch square tin and bake in a preheated oven, at 180°C/360°F/Gas 4, for 20–25 minutes.

Remove from the oven and allow to cool for a few minutes before marking into squares. When ready to serve, remove the squares from the tin using a spatula or palette knife. Serve with a large scoop of your favourite ice cream.

Menu 5

Gougère of prawns
Provençal

Sautéed green beans

Baked lemon pudding

serves 4

Gougère of prawns
Provençal

for the gougère
60 g/2 oz butter
150 ml/¼ pint water
75 g/2½ oz plain flour
pinch of salt
2 eggs, beaten
85 g/3 oz Emmenthal cheese, cut into 1 cm/½ inch cubes
1 teaspoon mild mustard
1 tablespoon chives

for the prawns Provençal
1 medium onion, finely chopped
1 tablespoon olive oil
2–3 cloves garlic, finely chopped
450 g/1 lb ripe tomatoes, peeled and chopped
1 small glass white wine
salt and pepper
340 g/12 oz prawns (peeled weight)
black olives and parsley to garnish

Choux pastry is very simple to make and can be used in many different ways, fried as in beignets (p. 82), or baked as in this gougère. There is a more detailed choux recipe on p. 176.

I like prawns cooked in a Provençal sauce to fill this dish but you could as easily use ratatouille or sautéed chicken livers.

In a heavy bottomed saucepan melt the butter in the water, bring to the boil, and cook for 30 seconds. Add the flour and salt, turn off the heat and beat the mixture well until it forms a smooth ball. Leave to cool for 5 minutes.

Beat the eggs into the flour mixture, a little at a time, using a food processor if you like, to make a glossy, fairly stiff mixture. Fold in the cheese, mustard and chopped chives.

Spoon the choux into a greased 17.5 cm/7 inch ovenproof dish leaving a space in the centre. Bake in a preheated oven, at 200°C/400°F/Gas 6, for 10 minutes, then turn the heat down to 180°C/360°F/Gas 4, and cook for a further 25–35 minutes or until the gougère is well risen and golden brown.

For the prawn filling, soften the onion in the oil and add the garlic. Cook for 2–3 minutes, then add the tomatoes. Pour in the wine, season lightly and simmer the sauce until it thickens, 10–15 minutes. Stir in the prawns and cook until heated through.

Serve spooned into the centre of the gougère. Garnish with chopped black olives and parsley.

Sautéed green beans

450 g/1 lb French beans
30 g/1 oz butter
1 large plump clove garlic, chopped
30 g/1 oz slivered almonds
salt, pepper

Top and tail the beans and cook them in plenty of boiling salted water for about 4 minutes. Drain, and if not using immediately, cool under running cold water and reserve.

When you are ready to eat, melt the butter in a wide frying pan. Sauté the garlic for 30 seconds, then add the beans and the almonds. Cook, stirring continuously, for about 3 minutes, or until everything is heated through. Season with salt and freshly ground black pepper and serve at once.

Baked lemon pudding

60 g/2 oz butter
grated rind and juice of 2 lemons
85 g/3 oz caster sugar
1 heaped teaspoonful plain flour
2 eggs, separated
200 ml/⅓ pint milk

Baked lemon pudding is best made in a food processor as the very high speed whisking stops the lemon from curdling the milk. Bake it in a bain marie, simply an oven tin filled with 2.5 cm/1 inch water, and serve warm or cool.

Using a food processor, cream the butter, lemon rind and sugar until you have a light mixture. Add the flour, egg yolks, lemon juice and milk, and process until smooth. In a large bowl, whisk the egg whites until stiff. Fold the lemon mixture into the egg whites.

Pour into a greased ovenproof dish and put the dish in a baking pan filled with 2.5 cm/1 inch warm water. Once you have turned the oven down to 180°C/360°F/Gas 4, put the pudding in with the gougère and cook for 40 minutes, or until lightly browned and set.

Menu 6

Flaky mushroom & feta pie

Mixed salad

Blackberry & fromage frais cups

serves 4

Flaky mushroom & feta pie

450 g/1 lb ready-made puff pastry
2 large Spanish onions, chopped
2 tablespoons olive oil
2 cloves garlic
4–6 large open mushrooms, sliced
85 g/3 oz feta cheese, crumbled
2 tablespoons white breadcrumbs
1 teaspoon dried, or 2 teaspoons fresh
   chopped thyme
1 large egg, beaten
salt and black pepper

If you holiday in Greece or on one of the Greek islands you will probably be offered borek – little cheese pastries sometimes filled with spinach, sometimes just with seasoned feta cheese, as part of an hors d'oeuvre or meze. I have expanded this idea to make a more substantial supper dish. Serve it with a mixed salad.

Fry the onion in the oil until it begins to colour, then add the garlic. Add the mushrooms and fry for 2–3 minutes. Tip the mixture into a large bowl and allow to cool for a few minutes, then add the cheese, breadcrumbs, thyme and seasoning. Reserving ½ teaspoonful for the glaze, add the egg. Mix everything together.

Roll out the pastry into an oblong 30 × 35 cm/12 × 14 inches and spread the filling over one half. Fold the other half over to make a pie, sealing the edges carefully. Brush with the reserved egg, thinned with a little milk, and bake the pie in a preheated oven, at 220°C/425°F/Gas 7, for 20–25 minutes.

Serve hot or cold, with a mixed salad.

MIXED SALAD

Greek salads usually have cucumber, onion, tomato and olives in them. You could serve hummus and pitta bread to start with if you want to expand the meal.

BLACKBERRY & FROMAGE FRAIS CUPS

450 g/1 lb blackberries
2–3 tablespoons honey
1 teaspoon arrowroot
225 g/8 oz fromage frais
1 teaspoon rosewater
sugar to taste
a few crystallized rose petals

I always keep a bag of frozen blackberries in the freezer. They are readily available from frozen food shops and make a refreshing change from raspberries.

Poach the blackberries in very little water with the honey until soft. Slake the arrowroot with a little cold water and stir into the fruit. Simmer for 1 minute to cook the arrowroot, then remove from the heat. Pour the blackberries into a shallow bowl and allow to cool.

Beat the fromage frais with the rosewater until smooth and sweeten to taste.

To serve, spoon the blackberries into four dessert glasses and cover with the fromage frais. Decorate each one with a rose petal.

MENU 7

CHICKEN & SWEETCORN CHOWDER

CORN, CHEESE & CHILLI MUFFINS

SPINACH SALAD

FRESH PEACH PIE

CREAM

serves 4

CHICKEN & SWEETCORN CHOWDER

340 g/12 oz boneless chicken meat, cubed
2 tablespoons oil
1 large onion, chopped
2 cloves garlic, chopped
2 ribs celery, sliced
2 leeks, well cleaned and sliced
2 carrots, sliced
1 tin sweetcorn kernels
vegetable stock
½ teaspoon fresh oregano
salt and pepper

to finish
1 tablespoon cornflour

Heat the oil in a large saucepan and fry the chicken until lightly coloured. Add the onion, garlic, celery, leeks and carrots, and cook for 2–3 minutes. Put the corn in a blender and whizz for 2–3 minutes to chop the kernels. Add these with the stock and oregano, then season lightly with salt and pepper.

Simmer the soup for 45 minutes. Mix the cornflour into a little water and then thicken the soup slightly with this. Simmer for 3 minutes to cook the cornflour, taste and re-season if necessary.

Chunky soups are very much the hallmark of America's East Coast, with the world's most famous clam chowder being made at an oyster bar on Grand Central Station.

I use tinned corn kernels, but should you have a fresh corn cob, do cut the kernels off and use those, as they will be even more delicious.

Corn, cheese & chilli muffins

85 g/3 oz Cheddar cheese, grated
1 green chilli, deseeded and chopped
140 g/5 oz plain flour
60 g/2 oz yellow cornmeal
2 teaspoons baking powder
½ teaspoon bicarbonate of soda
½ teaspoon salt
200 ml/⅓ pint milk
3 tablespoons oil
2 large eggs

Cornmeal muffins spiked with green chilli are wonderfully quick to make.

Mix all the ingredients together in a large bowl until well combined. Line 12–16 deep bun tins with paper cases and divide the mixture between them. Bake in a preheated oven, at 190°C/380°F/Gas 5, for about 15 minutes, or until risen and golden.

Spinach salad

washed young spinach leaves
1 tablespoon oil
115 g/4 oz streaky bacon, chopped
2 slices bread, cut into cubes
1 red onion, sliced into thin rings

for the dressing
1 tablespoon wine vinegar
2 tablespoons oil
1 tablespoon tomato ketchup
1 teaspoon sugar
Tabasco to taste
lemon juice to taste
salt and pepper

Tear the spinach into pieces and arrange in a bowl. Heat the oil in a frying pan and fry the bacon until crisp. Add to the spinach. Fry the bread cubes until crisp. Add with the onion.

Mix the dressing ingredients together by shaking in a screw-topped jar, and toss into the salad just before serving.

Fresh peach pie

450 g/1 lb shortcrust pastry
6 medium sized ripe peaches
1 tablespoon plain flour
1 teaspoon ground cinnamon
beaten egg, to glaze
2 tablespoons caster sugar

I have used fresh peaches in my pie but plums, apricots or blackcurrants would also be good.

Line a 17.5 cm/7 inch pie dish with pastry and re-roll the trimmings to make a lid.

Cut the fruit into pieces and discard the stones. In a large bowl mix together the flour, cinnamon and sugar. Toss the cut fruit in the flour mixture, then pile it into the pastry shell. Cover with the pastry lid, sealing the edges well. Brush the top with beaten egg and sprinkle with a little sugar. Bake the pie in a preheated oven with the muffins, at 190°C/380°F/Gas 5, for 34–45 minutes, or until the pastry is golden brown.

Serve hot or warm with cream.

MENU 8

TOMATO, MUSTARD & CHEESE TART

MIXED LEAF SALAD
with walnut oil dressing

CHERRY CLAFOUTIS

serves 4

TOMATO, MUSTARD & CHEESE TART

450 g/1 lb ready-made puff pastry
2–3 tablespoons Dijon mustard
170 g/6 oz Emmenthal, Gruyère or
    mature Gouda cheese, thinly sliced
5–6 large ripe tomatoes, sliced
salt and freshly ground black pepper

This is really one of the simplest and most delicious tarts I know. It is based on a French idea. You just cover thinly rolled puff pastry with mustard, finely sliced cheese and then ripe tomatoes. As always, the excellence of the finished dish depends greatly on the quality of the cheese and tomato used.

I would serve a simple mixed leaf salad with this tart, possibly adding some chopped walnuts and using nut oil in the dressing.

Heat the oven to 220°C/425°F/Gas 7.

Roll out the pastry to fit a pastry sheet approximately 30 × 45 cm/12 × 18 inches. Put the pastry on the greased baking sheet and spread liberally with the mustard. Cover with the cheese slices, top with tomato slices, season with salt and freshly ground black pepper and bake for 25–30 minutes, or until puffy and the bottom is brown.

CHERRY CLAFOUTIS

450 g/1 lb cherries

for the batter
85 g/3 oz plain flour
85 g/3 oz caster sugar
½ teaspoon salt
4 size 3 eggs
600 ml/1 pint creamy milk
1 teaspoon vanilla essence

Cherry clafoutis is a dish from the Limousin region of France. A rich batter is baked in the oven with the local tart cherries. Use pitted frozen cherries if you can find them when fresh cherries are not in season, or substitute peaches, apricots or dessert apples.

Butter a large shallow ovenproof dish. Combine the batter ingredients well in a food processor or blender. Put the fruit into the dish and pour over the batter. Bake in the oven, after removing the Tomato tart, at 200°C/400°F/Gas 6, for 50 minutes.

Serve hot or at room temperature.

Menu 9

Beef tacos
with salsa, shredded lettuce, cheese
& tomatoes

Chocolate mousse

serves 4

Beef tacos
with salsa, shredded lettuce, cheese
& tomatoes

450 g/1 lb lean minced beef
1 large clove garlic, crushed
1 teaspoon ground cumin
1 teaspoon dried oregano
¼ teaspoon cayenne pepper, or to taste
1 × 400 g/ 14 oz tin chopped tomatoes
1 × 400 g/14 oz tin red kidney beans

to finish
1 packet taco shells
¼ crisp Iceberg lettuce, shredded
2–3 firm ripe tomatoes, chopped
115 g/4 oz Cheddar cheese, grated
150 ml/¼ pint soured cream
fresh tomato and chilli salsa (p. 54)

*I love eating with my fingers, and this is
the only way to eat a taco.*

Cook the beef in a heavy pan until the
fat runs. Add the garlic and cook until
the meat is well browned. Add all the
seasonings and stir-fry with the meat
for 1 minute. Put the tomatoes and the
drained beans into the food processor
and whizz to chop the beans. Tip this
into the meat mixture, stir well and
simmer, covered, for 40 minutes,
stirring occasionally and adding a little
water if necessary.
 To finish, heat the taco shells in a
moderate oven for 5–10 minutes. Serve
the trimmings in separate dishes,
alongside a basket of warm shells and a
bowl of hot taco meat.

Chocolate mousse

170 g/6 oz plain chocolate
3 eggs, separated
1 tablespoon brandy

*Chocolate was first found in South
America, so a chocolate mousse makes
a fitting end to this Mexican meal.*

Melt the chocolate, either over a pan of
water, or in the microwave. Allow to
cool for a few moments, then beat in
the egg yolks, one at a time, and the
brandy.
 Whisk the whites until stiff and fold
in the chocolate mixture. (If the
chocolate mixture is a little solid, mix 1
tablespoon of the beaten whites in first,
then fold in the remainder.) Pour into
four glass dishes and refrigerate until
needed.

Menu 10

Broccoli & Sun-dried Tomato Quiche

Fennel & Watercress Salad

Brandysnap Sandwiches

serves 4

Broccoli & Sun-dried Tomato Quiche

170 g/6 oz broccoli florets
340 g/12 oz shortcrust pastry
6–8 sun-dried tomato halves
300 ml/½ pint single cream
3 size 2 eggs
black pepper

Deep red, intensely flavoursome and with a pleasantly chewy texture, sun-dried tomatoes are increasingly popular, and so easier to find in the shops. Most good food shops and Italian delicatessens should stock them.

Blanch the broccoli for 2 minutes in boiling water. Drain. Line a deep 20 cm/8 inch loose-bottomed flan tin with the pastry. Wash the tomatoes under running hot water for 30 seconds, drain and pat dry. Chop the tomatoes into large pieces and place them and the broccoli florets in the flan dish. Mix the custard ingredients together, season well with black pepper and pour over the vegetables. Note: the tomatoes are salty, so don't add extra salt to the custard.

Bake in a preheated oven, at 200°C/400°F/Gas 6, for 30–40 minutes, until the filling is golden brown and the pastry cooked.

Allow to cool for 10 minutes before serving.

Fennel & Watercress Salad

170 g/6 oz washed watercress
2–3 medium heads Florentine fennel
2 tablespoons extra virgin oil
2 teaspoons wine vinegar
salt and pepper to taste

The chewy tomato and the creamy custard in the quiche contrast well with the intensely green taste of the watercress and the lovely crisp aniseedy fennel. A good virgin oil should be used to dress this salad to keep the Italian feel.

Tear the watercress into pieces. Finely shred the fennel and toss the salad with the oil and vinegar. Season to taste.

Brandysnap sandwiches

85 g/3 oz demerara sugar
85 g/3 oz golden syrup
85 g/3 oz butter
85 g/3 oz plain flour
1 teaspoon ground ginger
300 ml/½ pint whipping cream
450 g/1 lb fresh berries
icing sugar, to decorate

Brandysnaps are so easy to make if you don't worry about rolling them round spoon handles! Here I have simply piled the crisp circles up into a multi-layered extravagance of cream, fruit and gingery biscuits.

In a medium saucepan melt the sugar, syrup and butter. Remove from the heat and stir in the flour and ginger. Drop dessertspoons of the mixture on to greased baking sheets, leaving plenty of space between them as the biscuits spread to about 12 cm/5 inches in diameter.

Bake them in batches in a preheated oven, at 190°C/380°F/Gas 5, for about 7 minutes, or until golden. Remove from the trays and cool on wire racks. The mixture makes about 16 biscuits; you will need 12. Store the rest in an airtight container.

Whip the cream and refrigerate until needed.

To assemble, place one biscuit on each dessert dish and cover with a little cream. Top this with a few berries, slicing them if necessary. Then put on another biscuit, more cream and more fruit. Top with a biscuit and decorate with a little icing sugar and a few berries.

MENU 11

ROAST CORN-FED CHICKEN

SWEET FRUITED RICE

SPINACH

FRESH PEACH & CREAM CHEESE SLICE

serves 4

ROAST CORN-FED CHICKEN

2 × 1 kg/2 lb corn-fed (yellow skinned)
  chickens
salt and pepper
3 red onions, quartered
3–4 plump cloves garlic
2 tablespoons olive oil
30 g/1 oz butter

*I love the flavour of yellow corn-fed
chicken simply roasted with butter,
olive oil, a few quartered onions and
some fat garlic cloves. Baste the birds
often while they are cooking and serve
with all the buttery juices poured over.*

Wash the chickens and season well.
Place them in a baking dish and tuck
the onions and garlic around. Pour over
the oil and dot with butter.
    Roast in a hot oven, 200°C/400°F/
Gas 6, for 50–60 minutes, or until the
juices run clear when a skewer is
inserted into the leg of the chicken.

SWEET FRUITED RICE

225 g/8 oz long-grain rice
a pinch of saffron strands
1 small glass white wine
2 shallots, chopped
1 tablespoon olive oil
450 ml/¾ pint water
1 stock cube
salt and pepper
85 g/3 oz sultanas
60 g/2 oz pine nuts

*This rice is not exactly sweet, but the
sugar from the fruit gives it a lovely
mellow flavour.*

In a long handled metal kitchen spoon,
toast the saffron for a few seconds over
a high flame, then crush to a powder
and mix into the wine.
    Fry the shallots in the oil for 2
minutes. Add the rice and stir to coat
with the hot oil. Add the water, the
stock cube, the wine and a little salt and
pepper.
    In a non-stick pan dry-fry the
sultanas and pine nuts until the fruit
swells and the nuts brown slightly, then
add to the rice. Simmer, partially
covered, for 20 minutes, or until the
rice is bite tender and the liquid
absorbed. Stir with a fork and turn into
a heated serving dish.

SPINACH

A brief word about cooking spinach. Wash the leaves very well, in several changes of water, as spinach is often grown in sand and can be very gritty. Shake most of the water off the leaves and pile them into a large saucepan. Put the pan on a high heat and cook the spinach in only the water that remains on the leaves, pressing and turning until they have wilted. Drain well, pressing out any dark juice, and serve with butter or cream and freshly grated nutmeg.

FRESH PEACH & CREAM CHEESE SLICE

6 fresh peaches
225 g/8 oz shortcrust pastry
170 g/6 oz low fat cream cheese
85 g/3 oz caster sugar
2 size 2 eggs, beaten
½ teaspoon almond essence

Not quite as rich as cheesecake, these slices are best made with fresh peaches.

Place the peaches in a bowl and cover with boiling water.

Roll out the pastry and line a circular flan dish 22.5 cm/9 inches in diameter. Beat the cheese with the sugar, eggs and almond essence. Spread this over the pastry.

Slip the skins from the peaches and slice, removing the stones. Arrange the slices over the cheese mixture.

Bake the tart at 200°C/400°F/Gas 6 for 35–40 minutes. Allow to cool a little before serving.

Menu 12

Chicken curry

Aloo bartha
(spiced mashed potato)

Fresh tomato chutney

Oranges in syrup
with cardamom cream

serves 4

Chicken curry

725 g/1½ lb boneless chicken meat
1 tablespoon oil
1 onion, chopped
1–2 cloves garlic, crushed
2 heaped teaspoons ground cumin
2 heaped teaspoons ground coriander
1 small green chilli, deseeded and sliced
2.5 cm/1 inch cube ginger, finely chopped
1 × 400 g/14 oz tin chopped tomatoes
salt, pepper

I love curries but since the advent of the real curry, I have found them rather daunting to prepare. Still, having tasted the real thing there is no turning back, so here is a simple one.

Heat the oil in a pan and fry the onion and garlic until lightly coloured. Add the spices, chilli and ginger and stir-fry for 1–2 minutes. Now put in the chicken and stir well, making sure the spices do not stick and burn. Pour in the tomatoes, season with salt and pepper, and give everything a good stir, scraping up any bits that have stuck to the sides. Bring to the boil and simmer, covered, for 35–40 minutes. If the sauce needs to be thicker, remove the lid and allow it to reduce slightly.

Aloo bartha
(spiced mashed potato)

450 g/1 lb potatoes
1 tablespoon oil
½ teaspoon black mustard seeds
1 green chilli, deseeded and chopped
1 small onion, chopped
¼ teaspoon turmeric
1 teaspoon garam masala
1 teaspoon salt
cayenne pepper to taste
1–2 tablespoons lemon juice
fresh mint, chopped

This recipe comes from a friend who has travelled and lived in Pakistan.

Cut the peeled potatoes into medium pieces and boil until soft, about 20 minutes. Drain and mash. Heat the oil and fry the mustard seeds until they pop. Add the chilli and onion and fry until the onion softens and colours. Add the turmeric, garam masala, salt and cayenne pepper, then stir and add the lemon juice. Add the mashed potatoes, mix well and heat through. Garnish with chopped mint.

Fresh tomato chutney

½ cucumber
salt
3 firm tomatoes
1 mild onion
juice of 1 large lemon

Dice the cucumber and sprinkle with salt, then leave to drain. Chop the tomatoes and onion finely. Rinse the cucumber and pat dry with kitchen paper. Mix the prepared vegetables together and mix in the lemon juice.

Oranges in syrup
with cardamom cream

6 medium oranges
30 g/1 oz caster sugar
150 ml/¼ pint water
4–5 cardamom pods
300 ml/½ pint whipping cream
sugar to taste

Most Indian meals end with fresh fruit, and so sliced oranges are appropriate. Flavouring the cream with crushed cardamom follows the lightly spiced theme.

With a sharp knife cut the peel from the oranges and slice into rings. Place the prepared fruit in a glass serving dish with any juice that collects. In a heavy bottomed saucepan melt the sugar and cook until the caramel is a rich brown colour. Carefully add the water; the caramel will bubble and spit. Stir well to dissolve any lumps, heating if necessary. Pour the syrup over the oranges, and refrigerate until needed.

Pick the seeds from the cardamom pods and crush with a spoon. Whip the cream until floppy, sweeten to taste, add the crushed seeds and beat until the cream holds soft peaks.

Serve the oranges with the cream.

Menu 13

CHICKEN PAPRIKA —
paprikas csirke

FRESH PASTA

GREEN SALAD

SLIPPED PANCAKES —
czusztatott palacsinta

serves 4

CHICKEN PAPRIKA —
paprikas csirke

4 large chicken breasts
2 tablespoons lard
2 medium onions, chopped
1 clove garlic
2 tablespoons sweet paprika
salt and pepper
300 ml/½ pint water
1½ tablespoons flour
150 ml/¼ pint soured cream

My sister is a very good cook and she gave me these recipes for authentic Hungarian dishes learned from her Hungarian husband's family.

Hungarian cooking is based on the slow browning of onions and garlic in lard and the use of sweet paprika. Paprika burns quickly, ruining the flavour of the finished dish, so remove the pan from the heat before you stir in this delicate spice.

Brown the chicken breasts in the lard in a frying pan. Remove and reserve. Fry the onions and garlic slowly in the hot fat, stirring occasionally, for about 10 minutes.

Remove from the heat and stir in the paprika, add salt and pepper and the water. Stir well, replace the chicken breasts and bring to the boil. Simmer, partially covered, for 30 minutes. Remove the chicken breasts and keep warm.

Mix the flour into the cream and stir into the paprika sauce until well blended. Cook the sauce for a further 2–3 minutes until thick and no raw flour taste remains. Whizz the sauce in a blender until smooth, taste, adjusting seasoning, and pour over the chicken.

Serve with fresh boiled pasta and a green salad.

SLIPPED PANCAKES —
csusztatott palacsinta

60 g/2 oz butter, softened
150 g/5½ oz plain flour
60 g/2 oz caster sugar
600 ml/1 pint milk
3 eggs, separated
1 teaspoon vanilla essence
115 g/4 oz butter, for cooking

for the filling
115 g/4 oz ground almonds
115 g/4 oz caster sugar

Slipped pancakes are a little fiddly to make but they are ambrosial to eat and so deserve inclusion here. Once the chicken is simmering you can concentrate on frying and stacking these light soufflé pancakes.

In a food processor beat the butter, flour, sugar, milk, egg yolks, and vanilla until smooth.

In a large bowl whip the egg whites until stiff and then fold in the batter. Mix the filling ingredients together.

Heat a 20 cm/8 inch frying pan and when hot put in a large knob of butter. As soon as the butter has melted pour in about 5 mm/¼ inch pancake batter. Cook the pancake over a medium heat until the underside is golden brown and bubbles are rising to the surface. Slide the pancake, cooked side down, on to the serving plate and sprinkle with a tablespoon of the almond/sugar mixture.

Continue until all the batter is used. When making the last pancake, turn to cook both sides. Sprinkle any remaining almond/sugar mixture over the stack and keep warm in a low oven until ready to serve.

Menu 14

Gammon, chicken & mushroom turnovers

Mixed baby vegetables

Blackberry & apple crumble

Hot spiced cream

serves 4

Gammon, chicken & mushroom turnovers

340 g/12 oz gammon steaks
285 g/10 oz boneless chicken meat
onion, carrot and bayleaf to cook
30 g/1 oz butter
1 shallot, chopped
30 g/1 oz flour
450 ml/¾ pint milk
150 ml/¼ pint cooking liquor
115 g/4 oz mushrooms
450 g/1 lb ready-made puff pastry
beaten egg, to glaze
sesame seeds, for sprinkling

These turnovers are delicious hot, but if you make two extra they are also very good cold as a packed lunch the following day. Serve them with a mixture of baby vegetables, which can now be bought from most high street supermarkets. Either microwave them in cook-bags or immerse in rapidly boiling water for 5 minutes.

Put the meats in a saucepan with the flavouring ingredients and simmer for 15 minutes. Remove, reserving the liquor, and allow to cool.

Melt the butter in a saucepan and fry the shallot for 2 minutes, add the flour and make a white sauce using the milk and a little cooking liquor. Allow the sauce to cool while you prepare the apple crumble.

To finish the turnovers, chop the mushrooms and the meat and stir into the sauce. Roll out the pastry and cut six 15 cm/6 inch squares. Divide the filling between them. Turn over one side of each square to form triangles, dampen and seal the edges. Brush with beaten egg and sprinkle with sesame seeds.

Bake in a preheated over, at 220°C/425°F/Gas 7, for 20–25 minutes.

BLACKBERRY & APPLE CRUMBLE

3 large Bramley apples
225 g/8 oz blackberries
60 g/2 oz butter
140 g/5 oz plain flour
60 g/2 oz soft brown sugar
1 generous teaspoon mixed spice

Peel and slice the apples and place with the berries in a suitable dish.

Rub the butter into the flour – this can be done in a food processor using a series of short bursts of power – and then add the sugar and spice.

Sprinkle this mixture over the fruit and bake in the oven, turning the heat down to 180°C/360°F/Gas 4, once you have removed the turnovers.

Serve with Hot spiced cream, right.

HOT SPICED CREAM

300 ml/½ pint double cream
2 teaspoons cinnamon
2 teaspoons ginger
2 tablespoons soft brown sugar

Put everything into a non-stick saucepan and simmer, stirring constantly, for 2–3 minutes, until the cream is hot and thickens slightly.

MENU 15

ROAST GROUSE
with white currants

FRIED CRUMBS

SPROUTS IN CREAM

POACHED PLUMS
with caramelized almonds

GREEK YOGHURT

serves 4

ROAST GROUSE
with white currants

1 plump young grouse per person
170 g/6 oz butter
225 g/8 oz white currants
salt and pepper
olive oil
flour, for dredging
1 glass dry sherry
300 ml/½ pint stock

The first game bird to arrive on the table each year, grouse is also one of the most expensive.

Here young birds stuffed with butter and white currants are quickly roasted, producing an excellent combination of rich meat and tart fruit.

Mash the butter with the white currants, reserving a few for garnish. Stuff the cleaned bird with this mixture and season well. Place the grouse in a roasting dish, pour over 1 tablespoon olive oil per bird and dredge with flour.

Roast in a preheated oven, at 220°C/425°F/Gas 7, for 10 minutes, turn the heat down to 180°C/360°F/Gas 4, and roast for a further 10–15 minutes. Baste the birds with the pan juices from time to time.

Remove the grouse from the tin and allow to stand in a warm oven while you make the sauce. Pour off most of the fat and then add the sherry. Put the pan over a medium heat and let the sherry bubble, stirring to scrape up any bits that have stuck to the pan, then add the stock and boil until the sauce has reduced and the taste is balanced.

Serve the grouse on a warm plate with a few fried crumbs (opposite) and a spoonful of sauce. Hand the rest of the sauce and crumbs separately, with the sprouts.

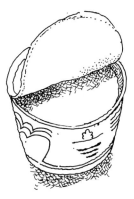

Fried crumbs

**115 g/4 oz fresh white or brown
  breadcrumbs
2 tablespoons olive oil
2 tablespoons butter
garlic or garlic salt**

Heat the oil and butter in a frying pan
and fry the crumbs over a low to
moderate heat until they are crisp,
stirring often. This will take 5–10
minutes. I prefer to season the crumbs
with garlic salt but you may fry a
crushed clove of garlic with the crumbs,
instead.

Sprouts in cream

*Stir-frying shredded sprouts and then
adding cream and lots of nutmeg is an
idea suggested to me by my friend and
colleague Trevor Grove. A keen cook,
Trevor likes to think that men show
extra flair in the kitchen as their
aptitude for science leads them to be
more experimental. While continuing to
contest this theory I must concede his
creativity in the kitchen.*

Poached plums
with caramelized almonds

**725 g/1½ lb dessert plums
1 cinnamon stick
75 ml/⅛ pint water
caster sugar to taste
1 tablespoon butter
2 tablespoons caster sugar
60 g/2 oz slivered almonds
225 g/8 oz Greek yoghurt**

Cut the plums in half and put into a
saucepan with the cinnamon stick,
water and a little sugar. Cook over a
low heat until the sugar dissolves, and
then simmer gently until the plums are
soft, 8–10 minutes. Place in a serving
dish. In a frying pan melt the butter
with the sugar and cook the almonds
until they colour and the sugar
caramelizes. Turn on to a greased
baking sheet and allow to cool.
  To serve, put the yoghurt in a serving
dish, separate the almonds into small
clusters and sprinkle over the yoghurt.
Serve with the plums.

Menu 16

Ceviche of Salmon
in orange & mint marinade

Honey roasted quail

Wild rice
with pine nuts & black olives

Cheese & fruit

serves 4

Ceviche of Salmon
in orange & mint marinade

225 g/8 oz very fresh salmon, skin and bones removed
juice of 1 large lemon
juice of 2 blood oranges
1 tablespoon chopped fresh mint leaves
pinch of caster sugar
salt and black pepper
a few whole mint leaves to garnish

This is an elegant meal suitable for entertaining. The salmon is marinated in fresh orange juice. If you can find sharp blood oranges with their vibrant red juice, do use those.

With a very sharp knife slice the salmon as thinly as possible (or get the fishmonger to do it for you). Arrange the fish in a single layer in a serving dish. Mix the marinade ingredients together and pour over the fish. Refrigerate until needed, at least 40 minutes.

Honey roasted quail

4–6 ovenready quail, according to appetites
salt and black pepper
3 tablespoons olive oil
1 medium onion, finely chopped
1 large glass dry white wine
6 fresh sage leaves
1 tablespoon flower honey

Quail are now available from many supermarkets and most fishmongers. Use a deep, lidded pan to 'roast' the birds and serve with wild rice, and possibly some steamed beans or courgettes.

Wash and dry the quail, then season with salt and pepper. Heat the oil in a deep frying pan with a lid, and brown the birds on all sides. Remove the quail from the pan and brown the onion, then replace the quail and pour over the wine, add the torn sage leaves and bring up to a simmer. Cover and simmer the quail for 15 minutes.

   Remove the lid and stir in the honey. Turn up the heat and reduce the sauce until it has thickened, basting the quail often. Serve with wild rice pilaf (opposite).

WILD RICE
with pine nuts & black olives

**225 g/8 oz mixed wild and long-grain
  rice**
600 ml/1 pint water
salt and pepper
1 large clove garlic, chopped
1 tablespoon olive oil
30 g/1 oz pine nut kernels
60 g/2 oz pitted black olives

*Marks and Spencer sell a mix of wild
and long-grain rice. Otherwise mix
30 g/1 oz wild rice with 190 g/7 oz
long-grain rice.*

Bring the rice to the boil in the water,
salt slightly, and simmer for 20 minutes
or until bite tender. Drain and keep hot.
   In a frying pan fry the garlic in the oil
with the pine nuts until light brown,
add the olives and toss them with the
nuts, stirring constantly, until they have
warmed through. Mix into the rice and
season to taste with salt and pepper.

CHEESE & FRUIT

*After this meal I would serve some ripe
unpasteurized Brie, a good medium
mature goats cheese and either ripe
fresh pears or muscatel grapes.*

Menu 17

Roast cured loin of pork

Cumberland sauce

Roast new potatoes

Baked amaretti-stuffed peaches

serves 4

Roast cured loin of pork

450 g/1 lb joint cured loin of pork
2 tablespoons orange marmalade
black pepper
1 bay leaf
2 tablespoons white wine

Cured loin of pork joints may look small, but they produce lean slices of good flavoured meat. I often bake two at once and keep one to serve cold with jacket potatoes and salad.

Prepare a large double thickness square of foil and place the joint of pork on this. Spoon the marmalade over the meat, add a grinding of black pepper, pop the bay leaf on top and then pour over the wine. Gather up the foil and wrap the meat loosely, making sure the seams are well sealed.

Bake in a preheated oven, at 190°C/380°F/Gas 5, for 45 minutes. Remove the ham from the foil and keep warm while you make the sauce.

Cumberland sauce

½ jar redcurrant jelly
3 tablespoons fresh orange juice
½ teaspoon English mustard
juices from the ham

Melt the jelly with the remaining ingredients in a small saucepan. Whisk to thoroughly combine the sauce and simmer for 3–4 minutes to reduce slightly. The sauce will be thin.

Roast new potatoes

450 g/1 lb new potatoes
2 tablespoons olive oil
1 teaspoon dried mixed herbs
salt and black pepper

These new potatoes are roasted in their skins. If you can't get hold of small potatoes, simply cut larger ones into wedges.

Wash and dry the potatoes and cut into thick wedges if necessary. Mix the oil and seasoning in a deep bowl and toss the potatoes in this, making sure all sides are coated.

Pour everything into a roasting pan and roast in the oven, at 190°C/380°F/Gas 5, for about 50 minutes, or until golden and crunchy.

Baked Amaretti-stuffed peaches

4 large fresh peaches, or 8 large peach halves
6 Amaretti biscuits
45 g/1½ oz butter
a small glass white wine

While I prefer to stuff fresh peaches, large tinned peach halves are dramatically improved by this lovely stuffing. Though they have a deceptively almond flavour, Amaretti biscuits are not made with almonds, but with apricot kernels.

Cover the peaches with boiling water for 1–2 minutes and then remove the skin. Slice the peaches in half, remove the stones and place cavity side up in a baking dish.

Crush the biscuits and mix to a paste with the butter. Stuff the peaches with this mixture. Pour the wine into the dish and bake in a medium oven, at 190°C/380°F/Gas 5, for 15–20 minutes, basting once or twice.

Menu 18

Pork & Apricot Bake

Crisp Boiled Cabbage

Brandied Apple Meringue

serves 4

Pork & Apricot Bake

450 g/1 lb pork fillet
salt and pepper
2 tablespoons olive oil
1 medium onion, chopped
1 plump clove garlic
1 red pepper, cubed
2 carrots, sliced
2 ribs celery, sliced
225 g/8 oz fresh pumpkin, cubed (if available)
60 g/2 oz dried apricots, quartered
600 ml/1 pint light stock
1 teaspoon arrowroot

to finish
85 g/3 oz brown breadcrumbs
2 tablespoons olive oil
1 clove garlic

This is a lovely autumn dish and if it's available I like to add some fresh pumpkin, cubed and peeled. I have used fillet of pork here as this needs very little cooking, though you can use less expensive leg of pork and increase the cooking time to 1 hour.

Season the pork well, heat the oil in a heavy casserole dish and fry the meat on all sides until browned. Add the onion and garlic, and cook until coloured. Add the prepared vegetables, the apricots and the stock. Bring to the boil and place in a preheated oven, at 180°C/360°F/Gas 4, for 40 minutes.

Meanwhile, fry the breadcrumbs in the oil with the crushed garlic until the crumbs are crisp.

When the meat is cooked, remove the casserole from the oven and place on the hob over a medium heat.

Slake the arrowroot with 2 tablespoons water and mix into the casserole. Stir well and cook until the sauce has thickened and no raw taste remains.

Transfer to a clean heated serving dish and sprinkle over the garlic crumbs.

CRISP BOILED CABBAGE

When cooking cabbage a few rules will make sure that dreaded memories of school dinners don't come rushing back.

☐ Wash the cabbage well, but don't slice it until just before cooking.
☐ Always use a large saucepan to allow plenty of room for the cabbage to boil.
☐ Slice the cabbage finely and cook over a high heat, in plenty of boiling, lightly salted water, for about 5 minutes.
☐ Drain well.
☐ Melt a large knob of butter in the saucepan while the cabbage drains and then toss the cabbage in the butter, seasoning with black pepper or nutmeg.

BRANDIED APPLE MERINGUE

3 large cooking apples
2 eggs, separated
1–2 tablespoons marmalade, or 1–2
    tablespoons sugar
1 tablespoon brandy
85 g/3 oz caster sugar

Brandied apple meringue is a light and delicate dessert that transform apples from the autumn glut into something quite delicious.

Peel, core and chop the apples and cook in very little water until the fruit is soft and you have a thick purée.

Allow to cool for a few minutes, then beat in the egg yolks, either the marmalade or sugar to taste, and the brandy. Pile the mixture into an ovenproof dish. Whisk the egg whites until stiff and then whisk in the sugar. When the mixture is very stiff, spoon the meringue over the purée.

Bake the meringue in the oven at 180°C/360°F/Gas 4 for 20 minutes. Serve hot or warm.

Menu 19

Garlic & herb seasoned
PORK CHOPS
baked on potatoes

Sweet & sour red cabbage

Marmalade crumble cake

Soured cream

serves 4

Garlic & herb seasoned pork chops
baked on potatoes

725 g/1½ lb potatoes
4 thick pork chops
1 tablespoon olive oil
1 teaspoon dried herbes de Provence
2 plump cloves garlic, chopped
600 ml/1 pint light stock
salt and pepper

As a weekend meal you can replace the chops with a joint of pork, increasing the cooking time accordingly.

Peel and slice the potatoes 3mm/⅛ inch thick. Place them in a bowl of cold water for 5 minutes.

Brush the chops with oil and cover with the dried herbs.

Drain the potatoes and arrange with the garlic in a shallow layer in a cast iron gratin dish. Pour over the stock and place the chops on top. Season well with salt and pepper and pour over any remaining oil.

Bake the dish for 50 minutes, turning the chops once and basting if necessary.

Sweet & sour red cabbage

1 small onion
30 g/1 oz butter
340 g/12 oz red cabbage, finely sliced
1 sweet apple, peeled and cored
1 tablespoon vinegar
2 tablespoons water
1 tablespoon brown sugar

The red cabbage can be cooked either in the oven or on the stove, depending on space.

In a heavy saucepan, fry the onion in the butter until soft. Add the remaining ingredients. Cover and put over a very low heat to cook for 40–50 minutes. Stir occasionally, adding water if necessary to stop the cabbage sticking.

Marmalade crumble cake

85 g/3 oz butter
170 g/6 oz self-raising flour
½ teaspoon baking powder
60 g/2 oz caster sugar
1 size 3 egg, beaten
1 heaped tablespoon marmalade

for the topping
30 g/1 oz soft brown sugar
1 teaspoon cinnamon

Eat some of the cake hot as a pudding with lashings of soured cream, and then store the remainder in an airtight tin for tea time.

In a food processor, process the butter, flour, baking powder and sugar until you have fine crumbs. Remove a quarter of the mixture and reserve. Mix the remaining mixture to a soft dropping consistency with the egg and marmalade, adding a little milk if necessary.

Put the mixture into a 17.5 cm/7 inch shallow cake tin, mix the reserved crumbs with the sugar and cinnamon for the topping, and sprinkle over.

Bake the cake in the oven, at 190°C/380°F/Gas 5, for 25–30 minutes.

Serve hot with soured cream.

Menu 20

Venison Steaks
with gin and juniper sauce

Parmesan Soufflé Potatoes

Soured Cream & Raisin Tart

serves 4

*Note: cook the potatoes in the oven first,
then turn it down to take the tart.*

Venison Steaks
with gin & juniper sauce

4 venison steaks
1 tablespoon olive oil
3 tablespoons gin
1 teaspoon juniper berries, crushed
150 ml/¼ pint double cream
salt and pepper

*I love the taste of free-range farmed
venison. Stronger than lamb but much
milder than traditional venison, this
farm-raised meat is now available in
supermarkets.*

Heat a heavy bottomed frying pan and
add the oil. Fry the steaks quickly,
about 4 minutes each side, remove and
keep warm. Deglaze the pan with the
gin and stir in the berries. Add the
cream and simmer for 2–3 minutes,
seasoning to taste with salt and pepper.
Divide the sauce between the steaks to
serve.

Parmesan Soufflé Potatoes

450 g/1 lb potatoes
60 g/2 oz butter
60 g/2 oz fresh Parmesan, grated
salt and pepper
1 egg, beaten

Boil the potatoes in plenty of salted
water until soft, about 20 minutes.
Mash them with the butter and cheese
and season well. Beat in the egg. Either
pipe small mounds or drop tablespoons
on to a greased baking sheet, and bake
in a preheated oven, at 200°C/400°F/
Gas 6, for 15–20 minutes until golden
brown.

Soured cream & raisin tart

**285 g/10 oz ready-made shortcrust
  pastry**
300 ml/½ pint soured cream
2 eggs
60 g/2 oz caster sugar
½ teaspoon grated nutmeg
85 g/3 oz raisins

*Soured cream and raisin tart lightly
spiced with nutmeg makes a good
companion to the juniper spiked sauce.*

Line a loose bottomed flan tin with the
pastry.

Beat the soured cream, eggs, sugar
and nutmeg together and stir in the
raisins.

Pour into the pastry case and bake in
a preheated oven, at 190°C/380°F/Gas
5, for 30 minutes. Serve warm.

MENU 21

LIVER, BACON & SAGE SKEWERS

FRESH TOMATO SAUCE

SAUTÉED POTATOES

STRAWBERRY SHORTCAKE

serves 4

LIVER, BACON & SAGE SKEWERS

450 g/1 lb lambs liver, cubed
black pepper
115 g/4 oz streaky bacon (rinded weight)
a handful of fresh sage leaves

I like to use lambs liver for this simple tasty dish, as it has a good mild flavour and is much less costly than calves liver.

Season the washed liver with black pepper. Cut each slice of bacon in half and wrap a piece around each liver cube, tucking a sage leaf into each parcel. Thread the meat on to four skewers.

Heat the grill to hot and cook the skewers, turning as necessary, until the bacon is crisp and the liver cooked to taste.

FRESH TOMATO SAUCE

725 g/1½ lb ripe tomatoes
1 shallot, chopped
1 plump clove garlic
1 tablespoon olive oil
salt and pepper
1 teaspoon chopped fresh chives

Fry the shallot and garlic in the oil in a large saucepan.

Roughly chop the tomatoes and put into the pan, season with a little salt and pepper and bring to the boil. Cover the pan and simmer for 30 minutes.

Sieve the sauce and return to the pan. Simmer, uncovered, until the sauce is the desired thickness. Check the seasoning and stir in the chives.

Sautéed potatoes

**725 g/1½ lb potatoes, peeled and cut
into large pieces
salt and black pepper
2–3 tablespoons olive oil
1 large onion, thinly sliced**

*Sautéed potatoes used to be on every
restaurant menu before the year-round
appearance of tiny new potatoes, but
seem now to have fallen out of vogue. I
still love sautéed potatoes: golden and
crisp and pack-full of calories.*

Boil the potatoes in plenty of salted
water for 5 minutes, drain and leave to
cool for a few minutes. Meanwhile,
heat the oil in a large frying pan and fry
the onion until soft. Cut the potatoes
into smaller slices and fry in the hot oil
with the onions. Cook the potatoes
until crisp and golden on all sides, then
remove from the pan, and sprinkle with
coarse salt and freshly ground pepper.

Strawberry shortcake

**60 g/2 oz butter
140 g/5 oz plain flour
¼ teaspoon salt
1 teaspoon baking powder
45 g/1½ oz soft brown sugar
milk**

to finish
**450 g/1 lb strawberries
sugar to taste
300 ml/½ pint whipping cream
½ teaspoon vanilla essence**

*Strawberry shortcake is really the
American version of a cream tea: a light
scone and lashings of double cream
topped with fresh strawberries rather
than jam.*

Slice the strawberries and toss in a little
sugar.
   Rub the butter into the flour, salt and
baking powder. When the mixture
resembles fine crumbs, add the sugar
and mix in enough milk to make a stiff
dough.
   Drop tablespoons of dough on to a
baking sheet and cook in a preheated
oven, at 200°C/400°F/Gas 6, for 20
minutes, until golden brown. Cool on a
rack until needed.
   Whip the cream with a little sugar
and the vanilla. When ready to serve,
split the shortcakes open and pile in the
cream and strawberries.

MENU 22

SAUSAGES
with spiced green lentils

VEGETABLE SKEWERS

APPLE & ALMOND STRUDELS

CREAM

serves 4

SAUSAGES
with spiced green lentils

450 g/1 lb pork sausages
1 shallot, chopped
1 tablespoon oil
1 teaspoon cumin seeds
170 g/6 oz green lentils
600 ml/1 pint water
1 large or 2 medium tomatoes
salt and pepper

to finish
1 medium onion, thinly sliced
1 plump clove garlic, thinly sliced
1 tablespoon oil

Green lentils may be today's designer ingredient but I'm sure they'll still be around long after fashions change. They are delicious, especially when you add some crisp fried garlic and onion at the last minute.

Fry the shallot in the oil until it begins to colour. Add the cumin seeds and stir-fry for 30 seconds. Put in the lentils and water and bring to the boil. Simmer, covered, for 40 minutes.

Grill the sausages.

Peel the tomatoes by covering with boiling water and slipping off the skins. Chop, and add to the lentils. Season to taste and cook for a further 5 minutes.

To finish, fry the onion and garlic in the oil until crisp. Tip the lentils into a serving dish and pour the garlic, onion and oil mixture on top. Serve with the sausages.

Vegetable skewers

**725 g/1½ lb mixed vegetables, such as
    red or green pepper, onion, courgette,
    mushroom, aubergine, tomato
2 tablespoons olive oil
salt and pepper
1 teaspoon chopped mixed herbs**

*Use a variety of colourful vegetables for
the skewers.*

Cut the vegetables into even sized cubes
and thread on to four skewers, making
the variety as large as possible. Mix the
oil, seasonings and herbs together.
Brush the skewers with this mixture and
cook under a hot grill for 10–15
minutes, turning often.

Apple & almond strudels

**225 g/8 oz filo pastry
115 g/4 oz butter, melted
2 large cooking apples
60 g/2 oz raisins
60 g/2 oz slivered almonds
60 g/2 oz ground almonds
2 teaspoons cinnamon
butter, for brushing
sugar, for sprinkling**

*The recipe for apple strudels makes
more than four, so freeze the rest, or if
you're really hungry, eat two.*

Peel and chop the apples and mix with
the remaining filling ingredients.
   Keep the filo covered with a damp
cloth while you work. Take one sheet of
pastry and brush with butter, fold in
half and brush again. Place three
tablespoons of filling in the centre of the
sheet and then turn in the sides and roll
down the top to make a sausage-shaped
parcel. Brush with butter and place on a
baking sheet. Continue until you have
used all the filling.
   Sprinkle the strudels with sugar and
bake in a preheated oven, at
200°C/400°F/Gas 6, for 20 minutes.
   Serve with cream.

CHAPTER
4

Cooking
ahead

WEEKDAY MEALS MAY be rushed affairs, with the need for fast tasty food paramount, but weekends offer a different set of priorities. Though you may not be far away from the stove, you won't want to spend all your precious free time slaving over it, so here is a selection of recipes that can be made ahead or put to cook untended while you are away from the kitchen.

Most of these recipes will feed 6 people, to allow for the extra mouths that always seem to appear at weekends. Some are homely dishes, others more elegant.

I usually make double the quantity of soup and put half in the freezer for another day.

The vegetable dishes all take a little time to prepare, but once ready they are very untemperamental, and they all taste as good cold as they do hot.

Most of the puddings mentioned earlier in this book can easily be adapted for cooking ahead. The exception is ice cream, and so I am giving a selection of my favourite ice cream recipes here, along with that other useful standby, meringue.

I don't own an ice cream maker, though I have often used those belonging to friends and can recommend them for making some of the smoother ice creams and sorbets.

- ☐ Very good ice cream can be made by the old tried and tested method of freezing in the freezer and occasionally beating out the ice crystals.

- ☐ Using cream with a high fat content means that fewer ice crystals form, so I have used double cream throughout.

- ☐ Adding a final flavouring such as caramelized breadcrumbs, chopped nuts and chocolate chips also improves the texture of a homemade ice.

- ☐ Allow homemade ice cream to soften slightly before serving.

Chicken, vegetable & noodle soup

serves 4–6
2 meaty chicken legs
1 tablespoon oil
1 large onion, chopped
2 leeks, sliced
2 carrots, sliced
1 red or green pepper, deseeded and
  chopped
2 ribs celery, chopped
225 g/8 oz courgettes or spring cabbage
1 litre/2 pints water
1 teaspoon dried mixed herbs
salt, pepper
60 g/2 oz soup noodles or broken
  spaghetti

I used to make this delicious soup with packets of chicken wing tips, but for some unknown reason they have disappeared from my local supermarket. Do chickens no longer have wingtips? Now I use chicken pieces – slightly less economical, but they taste just as good.

Heat the oil in a deep saucepan and fry the chicken pieces until they are golden brown all over, turning from time to time, about 5 minutes. Don't rush this first step. Remove the meat from the pot and then put in all the vegetables except the courgettes/cabbage. Stir these in the hot fat over a high heat so they fry a little. Replace the chicken and pour over the water. Add the mixed herbs and season with pepper and a little salt.

Bring the soup to the boil and simmer for 30 minutes. Remove the chicken legs from the pot, allow to cool for a few moments and then remove the meat from the bones. Chop it and return to the pan.

Put in the courgettes and noodles and simmer for a further 10–15 minutes. Check seasoning and serve.

This soup freezes well.

Chilli beef soup

serves 4–6
225 g/8 oz minced beef
2 medium onions, chopped
2 plump cloves garlic, chopped
scant tablespoon oil
2 teaspoons powdered cumin
1 teaspoon dried oregano
¼ teaspoon cayenne pepper
3 teaspoons sweet paprika
1 × 400 g/14 oz tin chopped tomatoes
1 tablespoon tomato purée
450 g/1 lb tin baked beans in tomato
  sauce
1 litre/2 pints water
salt and black pepper

This hot soup makes a good start to a winter picnic; few things taste better on a cold touch line.

In a large heavy pan dry-fry the beef until the fat runs and the meat is well browned. Using a slotted spoon, remove the beef from the pan, leaving as much of the fat as possible. Fry the onion and garlic in this adding the oil only if necessary, until the vegetables are golden brown.

Add the cumin, oregano and cayenne, and fry for a few minutes over a low heat. Return the meat to the pan, add the paprika and stir well. Add the water, the tomatoes and the tomato purée. Either whizz the beans in a food processor to chop them, or mash with a fork, and then add these to the soup.

Bring the soup to the boil and simmer, stirring occasionally, for 45 minutes. Taste to check seasoning and serve.

This soup freezes well.

Carrot, orange & fresh coriander soup

serves 4–6
450 g/1 lb carrots, sliced
2 large onions, chopped
60 g/2 oz butter
450 ml/¾ pint fresh orange juice
salt and pepper
1 litre/2 pints light stock
1–2 tablespoons chopped fresh coriander
150 ml/¼ pint soured cream

Carrot soups are beautiful to look at and good to eat cold or hot. I have grown to love the full flavour of fresh coriander, but parsley or chervil can be used instead.

Fry the onions in the butter until very soft but not coloured. Add the carrots and fry for a further 3–4 minutes. Now pour in the orange juice, and season with a little salt and pepper. Cover the pan and simmer the soup for 40 minutes, or until the carrots are well cooked.

Liquidize the soup and return to the saucepan. Add the stock, check the seasoning, and stir in half of the chopped coriander. Simmer for 5 minutes. Chill the soup if serving cold.

Beat the cream until smooth.

To serve, ladle the soup into bowls, spoon over a swirl of soured cream, and sprinkle on a little coriander.

Tomato & tarragon soup

serves 4–6
1 kg/2 lb ripe tomatoes
60 g/2 oz butter
1 large onion, chopped
a handful of fresh tarragon, or 2 tablespoons dried tarragon
1 litre/2 pints chicken stock
salt and pepper
1 glass fino sherry (optional)

Fresh tomato soup is a far cry from the tinned variety. Sharp and tangy, this soup is mellowed by the addition of lots of fresh tarragon. Dry sherry adds depth of flavour. This soup freezes well.

Melt the butter in a saucepan and cook the onion until very soft. Roughly slice the washed tomatoes, leaving on the stalks, add to the pot and stir well. Put in half the tarragon, a quarter of the stock, a little salt and black pepper, and the sherry. Bring to the boil and simmer, covered with a tightly fitting lid, for 30 minutes.

Pass the soup through a Mouli or whizz in a processor, then rub through a sieve.

Return to the pan, add the remaining stock and tarragon and check the seasoning. Simmer for 5 minutes, then serve.

VICHYSSOISE

serves 4–6
**725 g/1½ lb potatoes, cut into 2.5 cm/
  1 inch chunks**
450 g/1 lb leeks, sliced
60 g/2 oz butter
1 litre/2 pints chicken stock
salt and pepper
300 ml/½ pint single cream
chopped chives

*Perhaps the most elegant of all classic
soups is this wonderful potato and leek
cream. A very versatile soup, it can be
served both hot and cold, and freezes
well.*

Melt the butter in a large pan and sweat
the leeks for about 5 minutes. Do not
let them colour. Add the potatoes and
cook, stirring often, for 3–4 minutes,
until well covered with the butter. Add
the chicken stock and salt and pepper
and bring to the boil. Cover the pan
and simmer over a low flame until the
potatoes are cooked, about 25 minutes.
  Using a blender or a food processor,
liquidize the soup until it is very
smooth. Taste and adjust the seasoning,
and stir in the cream. If serving cold,
chill.
  Serve with a few chopped chives on
the soup.

MARINATED VEGETABLES

serves 4–6
4 tablespoons olive oil
**225 g/8 oz leeks, cut into 2.5 cm/1 inch
  slices**
225 g/8 oz fennel bulb, cut into eighths
225 g/8 oz button mushrooms
115 g/4 oz celery, sliced
3–4 cloves garlic, sliced
1 bay leaf
1 teaspoon dried thyme
½ teaspoon black peppercorns
salt to taste
1 teaspoon coriander seeds
60 g/2 oz sun-dried tomatoes, sliced
300 ml/½ pint white wine
1 tablespoon balsamic vinegar

*These marinated vegetables can be
varied to include whatever is seasonal.
Choose a wide variety and a balance of
flavours.*

Heat the oil in a large saucepan and
toss all the vegetables in the hot oil for
3–4 minutes. They should be well
coated with the oil and beginning to
cook. Add all the remaining ingredients
except the vinegar. If the wine doesn't
cover the mixture add a little water.
Bring to the boil and simmer for 10
minutes (less if you like your vegetables
crisp). Remove the vegetables from the
pan with a slotted spoon and boil the
marinade to reduce by a third.
  Remove from the heat and allow to
cool for a few minutes, then add the
vinegar. Adjust the seasoning and pour
over the vegetables. Leave for 24 hours,
then serve at room temperature.

AUBERGINE & TOMATO GRATIN

serves 6
2 large aubergines
salt and pepper
1 tablespoon olive oil
1 onion, finely chopped
1 clove garlic, chopped
600 ml/1 pint passata (bottled sieved
    tomato)
1 teaspoon dried oregano
1 large egg, beaten
plain flour
oil for frying
85 g/3 oz Gouda cheese, grated

The recipe for this aubergine dish, a variation on a classical Italian theme, was told me by a friend's Italian mother-in-law. A formidable cook, she would regularly prepare half a dozen dishes for the family's Sunday lunch, plus any number of treats for the children.

This gratin keeps well and can be made ahead.

Slice the aubergines into 5 mm/¼ inch rounds and sprinkle with salt. Put in a colander to drain for 30 minutes.

Meanwhile, heat the olive oil in a saucepan and fry the onion until translucent. Add the garlic and cook for a further minute. Pour in the tomato passata and stir in the oregano. Simmer the sauce for 15 minutes.

Wash and dry the aubergine slices, have the egg in a shallow dish and the well seasoned flour in another.

Heat 1 cm/½ inch of oil in a wide frying pan. Dip the aubergine slices first in the egg and then in the flour until well coated, then fry, a few at a time, until lightly brown on both sides.

Have a gratin dish ready and spoon a little tomato sauce over the bottom.

As they are ready, arrange the aubergine slices in the dish, covering with tomato sauce when you have a full layer. Continue to do this until you have used all the aubergine and sauce. Sprinkle the grated cheese on the top of the finished dish.

Bake the gratin in a preheated oven, at 200°C/400°F/Gas 6, for 20–25 minutes, or until the cheese has coloured and the sauce is bubbling.

Serve hot or cold.

CRESPOU

serves 4–6

for the spinach filling
1 shallot, finely chopped
1 clove garlic, finely chopped
1 tablespoon oil
60 g/2 oz pine nuts
225 g/8 oz spinach
75 g/2½ oz Parmesan cheese, freshly grated
salt and pepper to taste

for the tomato filling
1 shallot, chopped
1 clove garlic, chopped
1 tablespoon olive oil
1 × 400 g/14 oz tin chopped tomatoes
2 tablespoons tomato purée
½ teaspoon mixed herbs

for the pancakes
140 g/5 oz wholemeal flour
2 size 3 eggs, beaten
1 tablespoon butter
300 ml/½ pint milk
½ teaspoon salt
oil for frying

This wonderful recipe comes from Provence. It takes a little time to prepare but is essentially simple to cook, and so delicious and colourful that though I hesitated about including it, I couldn't leave it out.

Crespou makes a wonderful picnic dish, or it can be gently reheated as part of a vegetarian meal.

You can use thick mushroom duxelles to replace the spinach filling.

To make the spinach filling, gently fry the shallot and garlic in the oil until they are coloured. Add the pine nuts and as soon as they are toasted remove from the heat.

Bring a large pan of water to the boil and blanch the spinach for 60 seconds only, then drain and tip the leaves into a bowl of iced water.

When the spinach is cool, drain it well and squeeze out as much liquid as possible. Chop the leaves and mix with the onion/pine-nut mixture and the Parmesan cheese, seasoning to taste.

To make the tomato filling, fry the shallot and garlic in the oil until soft, then add the tomatoes, the purée and the herbs. Bring to the boil and simmer for 20 minutes, until very thick. Season and allow to cool.

Make a batter using the flour, eggs, butter, milk and salt. Fry thin pancakes in a 20 cm/8 inch frying pan, stacking them interleaved with greaseproof paper. You will need 7 pancakes.

To assemble the Crespou, place one pancake on a serving dish and spread with one third of the tomato sauce. Cover with a second pancake and spread with one third of the spinach mixture. Continue to do this until you have used all the filling and end with a plain pancake. Cover with a piece of greaseproof paper and then a plate, placing a weight on the plate. Leave overnight before serving.

BAKED FRITTATA

serves 4
½ green pepper, chopped
½ red pepper, chopped
2 large mushrooms, diced
1 medium courgette, diced
1 medium onion, chopped
1 clove garlic, chopped
2 tablespoons olive oil
4 large eggs, beaten
225 g/8 oz ricotta or low fat soft cheese
3 tablespoons milk
2 thick slices bread, cubed
45 g/1½ oz Parmesan cheese, grated
salt and black pepper to taste

This Italian recipe comes via America and is excellent for both picnics and light suppers. Serve with a mixed green salad and crusty bread. Frittata can also be eaten cold.

Start by softening the vegetables in the oil for 3–4 minutes to drive off some of the moisture, then allow to cool. Beat the eggs, ricotta and milk together until smooth, then stir in the vegetables and the remaining ingredients.

Pour everything into a well greased 22.5 cm/9 inch springform tin and bake in a preheated oven, at 180°C/360°F/Gas 4, for 30–40 minutes, until the centre is set and the top lightly browned. Allow the frittata to cool slightly before slipping a knife round the edge of the tin and removing.

BROCCOLI & TOMATO LASAGNE

serves 6
60 g/2 oz butter
60 g/2 oz flour
1 litre/2 pints milk
salt and black pepper
1 bayleaf
450 g/1 lb broccoli
1 teaspoon mixed herbs
2 × 400 g/14 oz tins chopped tomatoes
190 g/7 oz 'no-cook' lasagne sheets
60 g/2 oz Parmesan cheese, freshly grated

A vegetable lasagne is so much quicker to make than a meat-based one. I like to use broccoli and tomatoes as they complement each other in taste as well as colour.

Make a white sauce using the butter, flour and milk. Season well and simmer with the bayleaf for 5 minutes.

Chop the broccoli into smallish pieces and blanch in boiling water for 1 minute. Drain and run under cold water to refresh. Mix the herbs with the tomatoes.

Take a deep oblong ovenproof dish and spread a layer of sauce over the bottom. Place four or so lasagne sheets on this, making sure they don't overlap, spread over a little more sauce, then half the broccoli, and then half the tomatoes. Cover with another layer of pasta, then half the remaining sauce, the rest of the broccoli and tomatoes. Put on the final layer of pasta and the rest of the sauce. Sprinkle the top with the cheese and season well.

Cover the dish loosely with foil and bake in the oven, at 150°C/300°F/Gas 2, for 1½ hours. Uncover and turn the heat up high for 10 minutes to crisp the top before serving.

This lasagne can also be cooked at 200°C/400°F/Gas 6 for 30 minutes.

GRILLED ITALIAN VEGETABLES

serves 6
3–4 courgettes
1 large aubergine
2 large red onions
3 large potatoes
3 red peppers
olive oil
salt and pepper

Grilled Mediterranean vegetables may be quite the most fashionable dish in London, but they are in fact a long-standing favourite in Italian households.

While you may use the grill on your stove, these vegetables should really be prepared on a heated ridged cast iron griddle pan.

First prepare the vegetables. Slice the courgettes and aubergine lengthways into pieces about 1 cm/½ inch deep. If you wish you may salt the aubergine, but I don't always bother.

Cut the onion into slices 1 cm/½ inch deep, being careful that the rings stay together.

Peel and parboil the potatoes for 5 minutes, drain, cool and slice.

Cut the red peppers into quarters and grill under a regular grill close to the element until the skin bubbles and turns black. Remove and cover with a damp cloth for 5 minutes, then peel off the skin.

Heat the griddle, and a few at a time,

cook the prepared vegetables, turning once. The raised parts of the griddle will slightly scorch the vegetables, giving an appetising look to the dish.

As each vegetable is cooked, arrange on a large platter along with the red peppers.

Drizzle the dish with olive oil and sprinkle with salt and pepper.

Sometimes I fill the centre of the dish with slices of mozzarella cheese and tomatoes scattered with fresh basil.

Serve warm or cold with olives, a plate of good Italian salami, some lovely ciabatta bread and a jug of virgin olive oil.

Flaky saffron fish pie

serves 4–6
450 g/1 lb white fish fillets
parsley stalks
bay leaf
salt and pepper
pinch of saffron
1–2 tablespoons dry sherry
45 g/1½ oz butter
115 g/4 oz shelled prawns
pinch cayenne pepper
30 g/1 oz plain flour
300 ml/½ pint milk
115 g/4 oz oyster mushrooms
115 g/4 oz leeks, chopped
450 g/1 lb puff pastry
beaten egg, to glaze

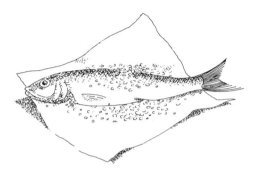

Fish is so quick to cook that it seems unnecessary to make too many fish dishes ahead. However, this saffron scented fish pie wrapped in puff pastry keeps happily overnight in the fridge and can be eaten hot or cold.

Cook the fish in water to cover with the seasonings until it flakes, then allow to cool. Remove any skin and bone and flake the fish. Strain and reserve a little fish liquor.

Toast the saffron in a metal kitchen spoon over a flame, crush to a powder, and stir it into the sherry.

Melt the butter in a non-stick pan and fry the prawns over a brisk heat until they lose some of their moisture. Remove from the pan and sprinkle with a little cayenne. Boil down the liquid left in the pan and when only the fat remains, add the flour and stir to make a roux. Make a white sauce using the milk, the sherry and a little reserved fish liquor. The sauce should be quite thick. Allow to cool.

Tear the mushrooms into pieces and carefully stir them into the sauce with the leeks, prawns, flaked fish and a little salt and pepper.

Roll out the pastry to form a sheet 30 × 45 cm/12 × 18 inches, pile the fish mixture on one half of the sheet and then turn the other half over to form the top of the pie. Brush the edges with water and press to seal well. Cut two vents in the top of the pie and glaze by brushing with beaten egg.

The pie can be covered and stored overnight in the refrigerator at this stage.

When you are ready to bake the pie, heat the oven to 200°C/400°F/Gas 6, and cook it for 40 minutes if the pie is at room temperature, or 50–60 minutes if cold.

Serve hot, warm, or cold with either a green vegetable or salad.

ESCABECHE OF SALMON

serves 4
450 g/1 lb salmon fillet (boned skinned weight)
4 tablespoons olive oil
2 shallots or red onions, thinly sliced
45 g/1½ oz shelled hazelnuts, roughly chopped
6 tablespoons white wine vinegar
60 g/2 oz seedless grapes, halved, or sultanas
½ teaspoon sugar
salt and pepper

Most marinated dishes need at least 24 hours to absorb the flavours of their marinade, and this escabeche is no exception.

Escabeche can be made from many different ingredients, including chicken, game and sole. I have chosen salmon, as it is available year-round and I love the mix of firm fish with the sweet sour flavour of the marinade.

Slice the salmon into 2.5 cm/1 inch strips and fry a few at a time in the oil. It is best to use a non-stick saucepan. When the salmon is golden on both sides, transfer to a serving dish, which should be big enough to take all the fish in a single layer.

Fry the shallots in the oil until softened, remove with a slotted spoon and arrange over the fish fillets. Fry the nuts for a few moments in the hot oil until they colour. Remove with a slotted spoon and sprinkle over the onions.

Put the vinegar, grapes or sultanas, sugar, salt and pepper into the pan and bring to the boil. Simmer for 1–2 minutes, scraping up any bits that have stuck on the bottom. Pour the marinade over the fish, cool and keep in the fridge for 24 hours, basting occasionally before serving.

ORIENTAL CHICKEN SALAD

serves 4
450 g/1 lb cooked chicken meat, sliced
1 small tin waterchestnuts, drained and sliced
4 spring onions, cut into 3 and shredded
1 red pepper, thinly sliced
170–225 g/6–8 oz beansprouts
4 pieces of crystallized ginger, cut into slivers
2 tablespoons sesame seeds
2 sheets Chinese noodles (optional)

for the dressing
4 tablespoons peanut oil
½ tablespoon sesame oil
juice of one lemon, or to taste
3 tablespoons soy sauce
1 tablespoon syrup from ginger jar
salt and pepper
cashew nuts to garnish

This chicken salad livens up ready-cooked chicken or leftovers from the Sunday roast.

Mix all the ingredients for the salad, except the Chinese noodles, in a large bowl. Combine the dressing ingredients in a jar and shake to mix well. Taste the dressing and correct the seasoning, then toss with the salad.

To extend this salad you can add the Chinese noodles. Bring a saucepan of water to the boil and put in 2 sheets of noodles. Turn off the heat and cover the pan. Allow the noodles to sit for 6 minutes, then drain and refresh under cold running water. Add the drained noodles to the salad.

Baked chicken in a brick

serves 6
2 kg/4½ lb chicken
salt and black pepper
1 large onion, sliced
1 clove garlic, sliced
450 g/1 lb medium sized new potatoes
3 tablespoons olive oil
1 teaspoon dried mixed herbs

Chicken baked in a brick was a common enough dish in the early '70s when we all rushed to stock up our kitchen shelves at Habitat or the wonderful Elizabeth David cook shop.

I'm sure that many of the chicken bricks sold ended up filled with geraniums on windowsills, but if you have one, they do provide a wonderful way of cooking both chicken and pork. To make a meal-in-one-dish I surround the chicken with potatoes tossed in oil and herbs and let everything bake together.

Wash the chicken thoroughly and season well. Place in the brick on top of some of the onions and garlic.

Scrub the potatoes, and if they are large cut into wedges. Mix the oil with the herbs and some salt and pepper and toss the prepared potatoes in this. Arrange them around the sides of the brick, with the remaining onions and garlic, pouring any extra oil over the chicken.

Place the brick in a cold oven, turn the heat to 230°C/450°F/Gas 8, and cook the chicken for 1¾–2 hours.

Remove the top of the brick and check the chicken is cooked through by inserting a skewer into the deepest part of the thigh. If no pink juice is seen then remove it from the brick and carve into portions. Arrange these on a serving dish and spoon over the liquor that has collected in the brick. Serve with the potatoes, and a green vegetable such as broccoli.

Pheasant
with lemon & rosemary

serves 4
2 medium pheasants, jointed
2–3 large cloves garlic, finely chopped
grated rind and juice of 2 lemons
3–4 sprigs fresh rosemary
salt and freshly ground black pepper
olive oil
seasoned flour
1 large glass white wine
600 ml/1 pint concentrated stock
225 g/8 oz carrots, chopped
225 g/8 oz celery, chopped
1 teaspoon arrowroot (optional)

This pheasant recipe is Italian in origin. The bird is jointed and marinated overnight in a mixture of lemon, garlic and herbs, then slowly cooked under a thick covering of chopped vegetables.

The night before cooking, combine the garlic, lemon rind and juice and rosemary, and rub the pheasant joints with this mixture. Put them in a shallow dish, season with salt and pepper, pour over 2 tablespoons olive oil, cover and leave overnight.

The next day heat 3 tablespoons oil in a frying pan, dust the joints with seasoned flour and fry briskly on both sides until coloured. Remove to a large gratin dish. Pour off any remaining oil and deglaze the pan with the wine. Add the stock, the remains of the marinade and a little salt and pepper, and bring to the boil. Arrange the chopped vegetables over the pheasants and pour over the stock mixture.

Cover loosely with foil and bake in a preheated oven, at 150°C/300°F/Gas 2, for 1½–2 hours. Ten minutes before serving, remove the foil and turn up the oven temperature to brown the vegetables slightly.

If you like a thicker sauce, carefully stir in the arrowroot, slaked with a little water.

PHEASANT
with sun-dried tomatoes & porcini mushrooms

serves 4
2 medium pheasants
8 sun-dried tomatoes
30 g/1 oz dried porcini mushrooms, or
   225 g/8 oz large open mushrooms,
   sliced
3 tablespoons olive oil
2 medium onions, chopped
2 plump cloves garlic, chopped
3 sprigs of fresh thyme, or 1 teaspoon
   dried thyme
1 large glass red wine (optional)

to finish
1 tablespoon arrowroot
chopped fresh parsley

I often buy pheasant at the end of the season and freeze them.

Even writing about this dish makes me hungry. It is one of my favourites, as it not only tastes wonderful but looks so rich and glossy. The robust sauce features both dried mushrooms and dried tomatoes, and the casserole can be served with creamy mashed potatoes or grilled polenta.

Put the tomatoes in enough boiling water and leave to soak for 5 minutes. Put the porcini in 600 ml/1 pint hot water and leave to soak for 5 minutes. Drain, reserving the liquor, and chop the mushrooms into large pieces. Strain the liquor through muslin or kitchen paper and reserve.

In a casserole large enough to take both birds, heat the oil and one at a time brown the birds on all sides. Remove from the pan. Fry the onion in the fat until lightly coloured and add the garlic. Fry this for 60 seconds with the thyme, then add the mushrooms, tomatoes and mushroom stock plus the wine if used, or extra water. Stir everything well, making sure any crispy bits that have stuck to the pan are incorporated in the sauce.

Replace the pheasants in the casserole and baste. Bring the pot to the boil, and when simmering, place in a preheated oven, at 150°C/300°F/Gas 2, and cook for 1½–2 hours.

Just before you are ready to serve the birds, take the dish from the oven and remove the pheasants. Carve each bird into several pieces and arrange on a heated serving dish. Slake 1 tablespoon of arrowroot with a little water and stir into the casserole juices. Simmer over a low heat for 1–2 minutes, until thickened, and then spoon over the prepared pheasant. Sprinkle over a little chopped parsley.

Wild duck pie

serves 6
2 large wild duck
olive oil
2 large shallots, chopped
1–2 cloves garlic
170 g/6 oz streaky bacon, rinded and chopped
1 teaspoon fresh thyme leaves
1 bayleaf
2 tablespoons brandy
600 ml/1 pint hot stock
400 ml/⅔ pint white wine
salt and black pepper
170 g/6 oz kumquats, sliced, or 115 g/ 4 oz dried apricots
450 g/1 lb ready-made puff pastry
beaten egg, to glaze

There is something rather comic about the name Wild duck pie. To me, it brings back memories of Desperate Dan and cow pie. However, this is elegant and appetizing food with which to feed family and friends.

The timing of pastry is of course critical, so if you must be away from the house until the last moment leave off the pastry and present the duck in a beautiful serving dish, sprinkled with lots of bright green chopped parsley and surrounded by garlic flavoured triangles of bread fried in olive oil.

As the ducks are simmered until tender don't worry too much about the age of the birds.

In a large casserole brown the ducks in olive oil on all sides. Remove and brown the shallots and garlic, add the bacon and cook until beginning to colour. Mix in the herbs, add the brandy and bring to the boil. Stir well. Put the ducks back into the casserole, pour over the hot stock and wine, and season with salt and pepper.

Cook in a preheated oven, at 150°/300°F/Gas 2, for 1½ hours, or until the ducks are tender.

Carve the ducks. Skim some of the excess fat from the sauce, and check the seasoning. You may need to dilute the sauce a little and then thicken it with arrowroot. If serving as an open dish stir in the kumquats, and cook for a further 15 minutes. Serve with jacket potatoes or rice.

If serving as a pie, mix the kumquats into the sauce and arrange everything in a deep dish with a lip. It is best to let the mixture cool at this stage. Roll out the pastry and cover the dish. Glaze with beaten egg.

Bake the pie in a preheated oven at 220°C/425°F/Gas 7 for 40–50 minutes.

PORK WITH PRUNES

serves 6

1–1.5 kg/2½–3 lb boned rolled shoulder
  of pork
170 g/6 oz ready-to-eat prunes
salt and pepper
2 tablespoons oil
115 g/4 oz streaky bacon, rinded and
  chopped
115 g/4 oz shallots, chopped
3–4 plump cloves garlic
675 g/1½ lb potatoes, diced
1 tablespoon brandy
150 ml/¼ pint white wine
½ teaspoon dried thyme
450 ml/¾ pint water

Another wonderful way of cooking pork comes from the southwest of France. Just to the south of the Dordogne lies the valley of the Lot river and it is here, in great orchards, that the plums for the world famous Agen prunes are grown. The French believe the prune to be an excellent fruit and treat it with great respect. They bottle it in brandy, make wonderful prune and armagnac ice cream and often serve prunes with pork.

Either open out the pork, stuff in half the prunes and re-tie or push in half the prunes from either end. Season the joint well and fry in the oil in a heavy casserole until well browned on all sides.

Remove the meat and fry the bacon until crisp. Remove. Fry the shallots, garlic and potatoes for about 5 minutes, until just colouring. Remove. Pour in the brandy and wine and stir up any bits that have stuck to the pan.

Now put everything back into the dish along with the remaining prunes, putting the meat on top of the vegetables. Season with salt, pepper and thyme and pour over the water. Bring to the boil, cover with a tightly fitting lid and place in a preheated oven, at 180°C/360°F/Gas 4, for 2 hours.

Serve slices of the meat with the wonderful bacon, prune and potato mixture from the casserole.

BRICK-ROASTED PORK
with lemon & rosemary

serves 6
**1.35 kg/3 lb joint boned rolled leg of
   pork
peel and juice of 1 lemon
4–5 sprigs fresh rosemary
salt and pepper
1 large onion, sliced
1 tablespoon olive oil**

*Leg of pork is also delicious roasted in
a brick. My mother makes deep cuts
into the meat and pushes in strips of
lemon peel and rosemary instead of the
more usual garlic.*

Wash and dry the pork. Thinly peel the
lemon, keeping the rind in long strips.
Make 4–5 deep cuts into the pork and
tuck a sprig of rosemary and a piece of
lemon peel into each one. Season the
pork well and lay it on top of the onion
in the brick. Pour over the oil and put
on the lid.
   Place the brick in a cold oven and
turn on the heat to 230°C/450°F/Gas 8.
Cook the pork for 2 hours, then carve
and serve with apple sauce and mashed
potatoes.
   The juice that has collected in the
brick can be served as it is or made into
a sauce by pouring it into a saucepan,
stirring in a little flour, and then adding
300 ml/½ pint stock. Boil the sauce for
2 minutes to cook the flour.

OVEN-BAKED SPARE RIBS

serves 6
1.3 kg/3 lb meaty pork spare ribs

for the marinade
**85 g/3 oz soft brown sugar
3 tablespoons Worcester sauce
3 tablespoons dark soy sauce
2 tablespoons cider vinegar
5 tablespoons tomato ketchup
1 teaspoon mild mustard
2 cloves garlic, crushed
300 ml/½ pint fresh orange juice
a good dash of Tabasco
ground black pepper**

*Pork spare ribs are a perennial favourite
at Chinese restaurants, but the portions
always seem rather meagre. Making
them yourself is simple – serve with a
crisp green salad and lots of hot bread.*

Mix all the marinade ingredients
together and pour over the ribs in a
deep baking dish. If you have the time,
leave them to marinate for 24 hours. If
not, leave them as long as you can.
Cook in a preheated oven, at
160°C/325°F/Gas 3, for 1½–2 hours.
Baste occasionally and turn once or
twice.
   When the ribs are very tender and the
sauce has reduced and become dark and
sticky, transfer to a serving dish.

Ham, beans & potatoes

serves 6–8
**1.5 kg/3 lb joint of mild cured ham or
    bacon**
1.5 kg/3 lb large potatoes
900 g/2 lb fresh or frozen French beans

*This is a good dish to have simmering
away while you work in the garden: a
hearty mixture of ham, beans and
potatoes simmered for at least four
hours and served with a good dollop of
garlic mayonnaise.*

*Choose the ham with care, as too
salty a piece of meat can ruin the
finished dish. To get rid of the salt, soak
the joint for 24 hours, changing the
water twice.*

*Serve the meat and whole vegetables
spooned into deep bowls with some of
the liquor. The meat should be tender
enough to eat with a fork and the
potatoes can be mashed into the juice.*

You will need a very large pot. Place
everything in the pot, cover with water
and simmer for 4 hours over a low heat.
Keep the lid of the pot just ajar and
check from time to time that the water
still covers the meat and vegetables.
    Serve with garlic mayonnaise, right.

Garlic mayonnaise

4–6 plump cloves garlic
¼ teaspoon salt
2 egg yolks
1 teaspoon mild mustard
black pepper
scant tablespoon wine vinegar
150 ml/¼ pint light olive oil

In a food processor purée the garlic
with the salt. Add the egg yolks,
mustard, a little black pepper and
vinegar and process well. With the
motor running, slowly pour on the oil,
drip by drip, to start with, then in a fine
stream, until all the oil has been used
and you have a thick pungent emulsion.

THREE-HOUR-BEEF

serves 4–6
**1 kg/2 lb stewing beef, trimmed and
cubed
115 g/4 oz butter
3 large Spanish onions, sliced
freshly ground black pepper**

*Three-hour beef is a very simple dish
that can be varied as much or as little as
you choose. In essence it is a mixture of
beef, onions and butter. You could use
a vegetable oil based margarine if you
wish, but butter does have a better
taste.*

*From this starting point you can add
beer – about 200 ml/⅓ pint; 225 g/8 oz
mushrooms; root vegetables up to
450 g/1 lb, red wine, and bacon – the
choice is yours.*

*If your casserole dish does not have a
tightly fitting lid, some of the naturally
produced juice will evaporate. To stop
this happening, make a flour and water
paste and use it to seal the lid. After
cooking, break the seal and discard the
hardened paste.*

In a large casserole with a very well
fitting lid melt the butter and lightly fry
the sliced onions until they soften.
Add the seasoned meat and stir well.
Cover the pot and place in a slow oven,
at 140°C/275°F/Gas 1, for 3 hours.

FILLET OF BEEF
with tarragon

serves 4–6
**1 kg/2 lb piece fillet of beef
2 tablespoons olive oil**

to finish
**a handful fresh tarragon
lemon juice to taste
6 tablespoons virgin olive oil
salt and black pepper**

*For a special treat buy a large piece of
fillet steak, roast it until just pink inside
and serve it cold with masses of
tarragon and virgin olive oil.*

Heat the oven to very hot,
250°C/475°F/Gas 9.
Wash and dry the fillet, season well
with black pepper and place in a
roasting dish. Pour over 2 tablespoons
of oil. Roast the meat for 30 minutes
and remove from the oven.
Allow the meat to cool, then wrap in
foil and refrigerate overnight.
A couple of hours before serving,
thinly slice the beef and arrange the
slices on a serving dish. Roughly chop
the tarragon and scatter over the beef.
Squeeze a little lemon over and then
evenly pour on the olive oil. Season
with salt and pepper.
Serve with rice salad or good crusty
bread.

Rakott krumpli

serves 6 or more
1.5 kg/3 lb potatoes
340 g/12 oz streaky bacon, rinded and diced
2 large onions, sliced
225 g/8 oz kabanos sausage, sliced
1 pork boiling ring or smoked Polish sausage, sliced
3–4 tablespoons sweet paprika
750 ml/1¼ pints soured cream
6 hardboiled eggs, chopped
30 g/1 oz butter
salt and pepper

This Hungarian recipe is a potato-lover's dream: layers of potato, soured cream, soft fried onion, egg and salami, with lots of paprika to add taste and colour.

Boil the potatoes in their skins and when cold, peel and slice 3 mm/⅛ inch thick.

Fry the bacon until the fat runs, add the onion and cook the two together until they soften and begin to brown. Add the kabanos and sausage and mix together in the pan. Remove from the heat and stir in the paprika.

Put 150 ml/¼ pint soured cream in the bottom of a deep earthenware dish and cover with a layer of potato, then cream, meat and eggs continuing in layers until you have used all the ingredients. End with a layer of potato topped with the last of the cream. Dot this layer with the butter and season with a little salt and pepper. The krumpli can be prepared up to this point a day ahead.

Cook the dish covered with foil in a slow oven, at 150°C/300°F/Gas 2, for 1½–2 hours, then serve with a green salad.

Note: should you wish, the krumpli may be cooked at 200°C/400°F/Gas 6 for 30 minutes.

Brown bread ice cream

serves 6
30 g/1 oz butter
30 g/1 oz soft brown sugar
85 g/3 oz brown breadcrumbs
600 ml/1 pint double cream
2–3 tablespoons caster sugar
1 teaspoon vanilla essence
1 tablespoon orange brandy (optional)

Melt the butter in a saucepan, add the sugar, and then the crumbs. Stir them together well and spread the mixture on a baking sheet. Bake in a moderate oven, stirring often until crisp and brown. Allow to cool.

Beat the cream until it begins to thicken, then add sugar to taste, the vanilla and brandy. The cream should be thick enough to hold its shape, but not solid.

Turn it into a suitable container and put into the coldest part of the freezer. Stir the ice cream two or three times while the cream freezes. Just before the mixture freezes solid, stir in the crumbs.

Chocolate chip ice cream

serves 6
300 ml/½ pint creamy milk
3 egg yolks
85 g/3 oz caster sugar
1 tablespoon cornflour, mixed with 3 tablespoons milk
1 teaspoon vanilla essence
300 ml/½ pint double cream
115 g/4 oz plain chocolate

Bring the milk to the boil in a heavy saucepan. Beat the yolks with the sugar and, when thick and light, pour on the hot milk. Pour this mixture on to the slaked cornflour and return to the saucepan. Cook the custard over a low heat until it boils, stirring constantly. Let the mixture bubble for about 60 seconds with the heat turned very low. Remove from the pan and allow to cool, stirring from time to time.

When the custard is cold, beat the cream until it begins to thicken, then mix it into the custard with the vanilla. Pour the mixture into a suitable container and freeze, beating the mixture twice, as it gets colder, to break down the ice crystals.

Just before the cream freezes solid, chop the chocolate roughly and stir the chips into the mixture.

Strawberry yoghurt ice

serves 6
450 g/1 lb strawberries, hulled and washed
115 g/4 oz icing sugar
1 tablespoon lemon juice
1 sachet gelatine
3 tablespoons hot water
225 g/8 oz Greek style yoghurt

Process the strawberries with the icing sugar and lemon juice in a blender or food processor until you have a smooth purée.

Sprinkle the gelatine over the water and allow to dissolve. Add with the yoghurt to the fruit purée and mix well.

Pour the mixture into a freezer dish and put into the coldest part of the freezer. When the ice is beginning to solidify, return the mixture to the processor and whizz for 60 seconds to break up the ice crystals, return to the freezer and freeze until hard.

Fresh pineapple ice

serves 4–6
1 large ripe pineapple
juice of 1 lemon
60 g/2 oz sugar, or to taste

Cut the peel, core and eyes from the
pineapple and liquidize it in a food
processor. Add the lemon juice and
sugar to taste. Pour the mixture into a
freezer dish and put into the coldest
part of the freezer. When the ice is
beginning to solidify, return to the
processor and whizz for 60 seconds to
break up the ice crystals. Return to the
freezer until hard.

Brown sugar & hazelnut meringues

3 large egg whites
85 g/3 oz caster sugar
85 g/3 oz light muscavado sugar
55 g/2 oz ground hazelnuts

Using an electric whisk, beat the egg
whites until stiff, add the caster sugar
and continue to beat until the mixture is
glossy. Then add the brown sugar and
beat for a further 2 minutes. Fold in the
hazelnuts and spoon the mixture on to
greased baking sheets.
    Bake in a cool oven, at 100°C/200°F/
Gas ½, for 1 hour or until crisp.
Remove and cool on a rack before
storing in an airtight tin.
    Sandwich together with whipped
cream to serve.
    These meringues are delicious if one
side is dipped into a little melted
chocolate and allow to set.

Pavlova

serves 6
3 large egg whites
170 g/6 oz caster sugar
1 teaspoon cornflour
1 teaspoon wine vinegar
300 ml/½ pint whipping cream
fresh fruit

*Australia's famous Pavlova can be
topped with whatever fruit is in season.
Alternatively choose a mixture of
chestnut purée and cream.*

Using an electric beater, beat the egg
whites until stiff. Add the sugar, one
third at a time, beating until the
mixture is stiff and glossy. Sift the
cornflour over the meringue, sprinkle
on the vinegar and carefully fold into
the meringue with a metal spoon.

Spoon the mixture on to a piece of
greaseproof paper on a baking sheet.
Shape the meringue into a 17.5 cm/
7 inch circle with a slight hollow in the
centre.

Bake in a low oven, at 140°C/275°F/
Gas 1, for 75 minutes. Allow to cool.

Carefully remove the paper and place
the Pavlova on a serving dish. Top with
the whipped cream and fruit.

The meringue will keep in the fridge
for up to 12 hours once filled.

CHAPTER

5

Entertaining

THE IDEA THAT food cooked for friends should be in some way different to food cooked for oneself is one that I've always found difficult to understand. Good food is good food, and I like to eat it every day. At my dinner table, when of choice I have at least eight friends, I try to serve simple delicious food that helps create a relaxed feeling, but doesn't daunt those wanting to return the invitation. If you cook to impress, you will either stun your guests into awed silence and ruin the evening, or your skill will go unnoticed in favour of the particularly juicy piece of gossip served up alongside your masterpiece.

At least two of the three courses should be easy to put together. Start with a selection of sliced Italian or French salamis, some ripe melon, fresh figs, a simple salad of baby leaves tossed in oil, and some slices of grilled duck breast.

Cheese and fruit make the ideal dessert to almost any meal. I would rather have one really good piece of cheese than a selection of thin and rapidly spoiling smaller pieces. If you like to serve salad after the main course, you can add grilled goats cheese and so combine these two courses. Luxury ice creams are now widely available and make a wonderful dessert treat for your guests. Suggestions for making your own ice creams are on p. 150.

Christmas is the height of the year's entertaining, and I have included my ideas for an alternative Christmas here, but please don't feel that you need to wait until then to try them out. They make excellent celebration food for any occasion, as do the simple but luxurious salmon dishes.

If you're throwing a party, provide enough food. The ideas here can be combined with various other recipes from the book to provide an appetizing selection. You could add the tomato, mustard and cheese tart (p. 104), tuna beignets (p. 82), and pizza (p. 24); and the risottos (pp. 36, 38 and 179) can be cooled, rolled into balls and deep-fried. Cocktail quiches can be made in bun tins, using the recipe on p. 106. Many supermarkets sell a range of prepared vegetables that can be eaten with the simply made dips.

At a party, always provide more than one drink. It's easier to offer only the host's own punch, but straight shots of fortified alcohol with floating fruit may be more than some can stand. Don't let the soft alternative be a box of unchilled orange juice. There are many different juices available now, or you could try elderflower cordial diluted with fizzy water, which is delicious. Alongside the wine, a selection of low- or no-alcohol beers and wines will be appreciated by those who are driving.

CHICKPEA & GARLIC SPREAD

1 tin chickpeas, drained
2-3 cloves garlic, chopped
juice and grated rind of half a lemon
115 g/4 oz cream cheese
salt and pepper

Whizz everything in a blender or processor until smooth. Serve with tiny crackers.

GUACAMOLE

2 ripe avocados
1 red onion, finely chopped
1 large tomato, peeled and chopped
1 dried chilli, crushed
salt and pepper
lemon juice to taste

Mash the avocado with a fork and beat in the remaining ingredients. Serve with tortilla chips.

POTTED CHEESE

225 g/8 oz cream cheese
225 g/8 oz mature Cheddar, grated
60 g/2 oz butter
1 teaspoon Worcester sauce
dash Tabasco

Whizz everything in a blender or processor until smooth. Serve with crackers.

Ricotta & black olive spread

450 g/1 lb ricotta cheese
225 g/8 oz stoned black olives
2 cloves garlic
salt and black pepper
small handful of parsley

Whizz everything in a blender until smooth. Serve with crackers.

Aubergine spread

1 medium aubergine
1 clove garlic
small handful fresh parsley
3 tablespoons olive oil
salt, pepper
lemon juice

Prick the skin of the aubergine and either bake, wrapped in foil, in a medium oven, for about 40 minutes, or microwave, unwrapped, for 7 minutes on high.

The aubergine should be very soft. Chop the flesh roughly and put with the garlic and parsley into a food processor. Whizz until everything is smooth, and then with the motor still running, pour in the oil in a thin stream. Season to taste with salt, pepper and lemon juice.

Tuna Pâté

225 g/8 oz canned tuna, drained
115 g/4 oz soft butter
salt and pepper
lemon juice to taste
a small bunch dill

Blend everything until smooth, and
serve on crisp toast fingers.

Nachos

Spread corn chips on a baking tray and
scatter generously with grated cheese.
Dot with small pieces of chilli pepper.
Just before serving, place under a hot
grill until the cheese bubbles.

Anchovy Whirls

1 small tin anchovies
225 g/8 oz puff pastry
black pepper

Mash the anchovies plus the oil in the
tin to a smooth paste. Roll out the
pastry as thinly as possible. Spread the
paste over the pastry and then roll up
firmly, sealing the edge with water and
pressing down well.

Cut the 'sausage' into rings about
5 mm/¼ inch thick and place on a
baking sheet. Cook in a hot oven, at
200°C/400°F/Gas 6, for 15 minutes, or
until crisp and golden.

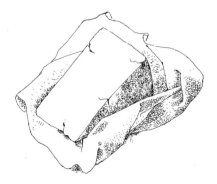

CURRIED CHEESE & MANGO CHUTNEY SPREAD

2 tablespoons curry sauce
225 g/8 oz cream cheese
½ jar mango chutney

Beat the curry sauce into the cheese and spoon into the centre of a bowl with a lip. Pour the chutney over the cheese, letting it run all over the mound. Serve with crackers.

EAST & WEST DEVILS ON HORSEBACK

1 large tin waterchestnuts, drained
1 tablespoon soy sauce
rinded streaky bacon
1 packet ready-to-eat prunes

Marinate the chestnuts in soy for 20–30 minutes.

Cut the bacon strips in half and wrap each piece around either a prune or chestnut. Thread on to skewers and grill, turning once or twice. Serve hot.

Bruschetta

Cut a rustic white loaf into 1 cm/½ inch slices and cut these into 2.5 cm/1 inch strips. Arrange on a baking sheet.

Meanwhile, crush 2–3 cloves of garlic into 300 ml/½ pint olive oil and season well with salt and pepper. Warm the oil and leave to infuse for 10–30 minutes.

Brush the bread strips generously with oil and, just before serving, bake in a hot oven, at 220°C/425°F/Gas 7, for 10 minutes.

Mozzarella, tomato & basil sticks

Cut mozzarella cheese into 2.5 cm/1 inch cubes and marinate in a mixture of olive oil, pepper and a little oregano for at least 30 minutes. Drain and thread on to cocktail sticks with a cherry tomato and a small piece of fresh basil.

Poached salmon

Salmon makes an easily prepared and delicious party meal. The crucial thing is not whether the salmon is farmed or wild, but how the fish is cooked. Overcooked salmon tastes strongly of fish oil, and is either pappy or rock solid. But lightly poached or baked salmon is quite delightful and feeds the five thousand with ease.

The best way to cook a whole fish is in a fish kettle. Simply place the fish in the kettle, cover with cold water, and throw in some sliced onion, peppercorns, coarse salt, bay leaves and lemon slices. Put on the lid and bring the water up to boiling point. Allow the fish to simmer for 1 minute and then turn off the heat. Allow the fish to sit in the water for 30 minutes if serving hot, or until cooled if serving cold.

If you are serving the fish hot, lift it out on the kettle tray, remove the upper skin, and invert the fish on to a plate. You can now remove the lower skin, give the plate a quick wipe and decorate it with some lemon or watercress. Nothing could be simpler.

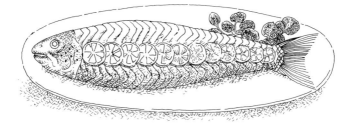

SALMON
in a puff pastry jacket

**1.3–1.8 kg/3–4 lb salmon, skinned and
  filleted**
1 kg/2 lb ready-made puff pastry
200 ml/⅓ pint soured cream
a bunch of dill
salt and pepper
1 egg, beaten with a little salt
sesame seeds

*If you do not own a fish kettle you
could try hiring one from your
fishmonger or from a local kitchen
shop, or ask the fishmonger to fillet and
skin your fish, and then wrap it in puff
pastry and bake it. The dish can be
prepared several hours ahead of
cooking.*

Wash and dry the salmon fillets.

Roll out two sheets of pastry until
they are about 5 cm/2 inches longer and
wider than the salmon fillets. Place one
sheet on a large greased baking sheet
and put one fillet of salmon on it.

Drain any whey from the soured
cream and place in the food processor.
Add the dill and plenty of salt and
pepper. Process to chop the dill into the
cream.

Spread the dill mixture on the salmon
fillet and place the next side of salmon
on top, reforming the fish.

Brush the edges of the pastry with a
little water and lay the second sheet on
top. Press the edges firmly together to
seal and cut two vents in the top. You
may want to trim the pastry around the
fish to give a fish-shaped parcel. If you
have leftover pastry trimmings you can
reroll these and cut some decorative
leaves.

Brush the pastry all over with the
beaten egg and sprinkle with sesame
seeds.

Bake the fish in a preheated oven, at
200°C/400°F/Gas 6, for 40–50 minutes,
by which time the pastry will be puffed
up and golden brown. Serve with
Beurre blanc (p. 93) or more soured
cream and dill.

This dish is also good cold with green
mayonnaise (p. 163) and possibly some
tiny boiled potatoes plus a green salad.

Green mayonnaise

300 m/½ pint good mayonnaise (p. 171)
1 bunch watercress, washed and dried
a small handful fresh parsley, washed
and dried

*If you are going to set the buffet
out in a warm room I would use a
commercially prepared mayonnaise
rather than one based on raw eggs.*

Place all the ingredients in a blender
and blend until smooth. Serve with cold
salmon.

Redcurrant & port sauce

1 wine glass port
pan juices
600 ml/1 pint stock or vegetable water
2–3 tablespoons redcurrant jelly
fecula or arrowroot to thicken
225 g/8 oz frozen redcurrants
salt and pepper to taste

*If redcurrants are unavailable, simmer
cranberries for 10–15 minutes in a little
water and add to the sauce after
thickening.*

Pour the port into the pan in which the
venison was cooked and give everything
a good stir, scraping up any bits that
have stuck to the pan. Add the stock
and bring to the boil. Simmer for 5
minutes, stirring and pressing the
vegetables with the spoon to extract the
flavour.
   Sieve into a clean saucepan and add
the redcurrant jelly. Now thicken the
sauce with slaked arrowroot or fecula
(potato flour) and simmer until the
sauce is glossy. Add the redcurrants and
cook for 2 minutes. Check seasoning
and serve.

Roast saddle of venison

**3.5 kg/8 lb saddle of venison on the
bone
2 onions, quartered
4 tablespoons olive oil**

for the marinade
**½ bottle red wine
1 onion, sliced
1 teaspoon juniper berries, crushed
2 bay leaves, crumbled
2 fat cloves garlic, chopped
4 tablespoons olive oil
ground black pepper
1 carrot, chopped
1 tablespoon crushed thyme leaves
grated zest of 1 orange
1 rib celery, chopped**

*Venison should be carefully chosen to
be young and tender. I prefer free-range
farmed venison and usually buy mine
from Pelham Venison in Hertfordshire,
a county which has a deep traditional
association with the deer. I would serve
this with Redcurrant and port sauce
(p. 163), Gratin dauphinoise (p. 165),
some tiny steamed vegetables or a
boiled waxy potato such as Pink Fir
Apple, and sprouts cooked in cream
(p. 116). Red cabbage (p. 124) is also
very good with this robustly flavoured
meal.*

Mix the marinade ingredients together
in a deep bowl, put in the venison and
leave to marinate overnight, basting
occasionally.

About 1 hour and 40 minutes before
you want to eat, heat the oven to very
hot, 230°C/450°F/Gas 8.

Place the venison in a large roasting
pan along with the onions and pour
over the marinade. Drizzle the oil over
the top and cook in the oven for 10
minutes to seal the meat. Turn the heat
down to 200°C/400°F/Gas 6 and cook
for a further 70 minutes, basting often.

The venison will be medium rare at
this stage; should you like it well done,
cook for a further 10 minutes.

Remove the joint from the oven and
put on a warmed carving dish to rest
for 15 minutes before carving.

GRATIN DAUPHINOISE

1 kg/2 lb firm potatoes
salt and black pepper
1–2 plump cloves garlic, crushed
600 ml/1 pint double cream
1 generous tablespoon butter

This is not as quick as most potato recipes, but delicious for a special occasion.

Peel and slice the potatoes about 3mm/ ⅛ inch thick. There is a special food processor blade that will do this, or use a mandolin, or a sharp knife. Soak for a few minutes in plenty of cold water, drain and pat dry.

Have a large earthenware dish well buttered. Arrange a single layer of potato in the bottom of the dish, season well, sprinkle on a little garlic and spoon over some cream. Continue to do this until you have used all the ingredients. Dot the top with the remaining butter and cover loosely with foil.

Bake in the oven with the venison for 1½ hours after you have turned the heat down to 200°C/400°F/Gas 6. Remove the foil for the last half hour of cooking.

CRANBERRY & ORANGE RELISH

1 thin skinned orange
225 g/8 oz frozen cranberries
sugar to taste

This is a super quick cranberry relish to go with the venison or a Christmas turkey.

Quarter the orange and remove the pips. Put the pieces into a food processor and chop. Add the berries and sugar to taste and continue to process until you have a thick relish. Store in the fridge.

Pork, Bacon & Chicken Liver Terrine

1 medium onion, chopped
1 plump clove garlic
1 tablespoon oil
170 g/6 oz streaky bacon, rinded and finely chopped, plus 4 extra strips
450 g/1 lb minced pork
30 g/1 oz white breadcrumbs
6 juniper berries, crushed
1 egg, beaten
¼ teaspoon ground allspice
1 teaspoon ground thyme
2 tablespoons brandy
225 g/8 oz chicken livers
salt and pepper
bay leaf, to top the pâté

At Christmas it's a good idea to have a terrine or pâté for people to cut into. This pork and chicken liver terrine is very simple to put together and takes only an hour to cook.

Store in the fridge for 2–3 days before eating to allow the flavours to develop.

Fry the onion and garlic in the oil until light brown and then mix all the ingredients except the whole bacon strips and livers together, seasoning well. Line a 1 kg/2 lb loaf pan with 2 strips of bacon, and spread on half the pâté mix.

Wash the chicken livers and remove any membranes. Lie the livers on the pâté and put the rest of the mixture on top. Top with the remaining 2 strips of bacon and add the bay leaf.

Cover tightly with foil and bake in a preheated oven, at 180°C/360°F/Gas 4, for one hour. Test the pâté by inserting a skewer in the centre: if the juices run clear the terrine is cooked; if not, return to the oven and cook for a few more minutes.

Allow to cool, then store, covered, in the fridge for 2–3 days before serving with crisp toast.

Warm Spinach, Raisin & Pine Nut Salad

1 kg/2 lb young spinach, well washed
2 tablespoons olive oil
4 medium carrots, coarsely grated
1 clove garlic, finely chopped
2 tablespoons raisins
2 tablespoons pine nuts

for the dressing
1 tablespoon wine vinegar
1 tablespoon olive oil
1 tablespoon tomato ketchup
½ teaspoon sugar
Tabasco
lemon juice to taste
salt and black pepper

This warm spinach salad offers a delightful vegetarian alternative to all those Christmas roast meats.

Mix the dressing ingredients together.

Arrange the spinach in a large salad bowl. Heat the oil in a wok and toss in the carrots. Stir-fry for 2 minutes. Add the garlic, raisins and pine nuts and keep tossing everything in the hot oil until the raisins plump and the nuts are golden brown.

Pour in the dressing, stir, and then pour the contents of the wok over the spinach. Toss and serve at once.

Prune, almond & brandy tart

285 g/10 oz shortcrust pastry
1 jar of prunes in brandy (see below)
300 ml/½ pint soured cream
3 egg yolks
60 g/2 oz caster sugar
60 g/2 oz ground almonds
45 g/1½ oz butter, melted
1 tablespoon brandy

This is a delicious creamy almond pie incorporating brandy-soaked prunes, which makes a good substitute for plum pudding. The pie can be made the day before and reheated. If you are unable to find prunes in brandy, make them, according to the recipe below, 3–4 days before needed.

Line a loose bottomed 22.5 cm/9 inch flan tin with the pastry. Drain the prunes and arrange in the shell. Either drink the liquor, or reserve it to use as a sauce for ice cream. Beat the remaining ingredients together well and pour over the prunes. Bake in a preheated oven, at 190°C/380°F/Gas 5, for 30–40 minutes until golden brown.
   Serve warm.

Quick prunes
in brandy

225 g/ 8oz prunes (choose the biggest available)
cold tea
1 tablespoon brown sugar
brandy

Cover the prunes with tea and leave overnight. Add the sugar, bring to the boil, and simmer gently for 2–3 minutes. Drain and put the prunes into a deep jar, then cover with brandy. Reduce the cooking liquid by fast boiling until you have 3–4 tablespoons. Add this to the prunes. Seal the jar and leave in a cool place until needed.

BRANDY-SOAKED SPICED BREAD PUDDING

190 g/7 oz wholemeal breadcrumbs
30 g/1 oz ground almonds
30 g/1 oz slivered almonds
60 g/2 oz chopped mixed peel
190 g/7 oz mixed fruit
1 tablespoon mixed spice
½ teaspoon freshly grated nutmeg
60 g/2 oz butter, melted
2 tablespoons brandy, plus extra
juice and rind of half a lemon
300 ml/½ pint milk
1 size 2 egg, beaten

Another alternative Christmas pudding, this is every bit as good as the genuine long-boiled article.

Mix everything together well and if liked leave in the fridge overnight. Place the mixture in a well greased fluted tin and bake in a preheated oven, at 180°C/360°F/Gas 4, for about 1 hour. When ready, turn out and pour over a little extra brandy which you may light if liked.

Serve with Whipped brandy butter or Spiced brandied cream (right).

WHIPPED BRANDY BUTTER

60 g/2 oz soft butter
115 g/4 oz icing sugar
brandy to taste

Using an electric whisk, beat the butter and sugar together until very light and fluffy. Gradually beat in brandy to taste. Pile into a serving dish.

SPICED BRANDIED CREAM

300 ml/½ pint double cream
1 teaspoon cinnamon
½ teaspoon ginger
1–2 tablespoons brown sugar
1–2 tablespoons brandy or rum

Warm the cream in a saucepan with the spices. Bring up to the boil and sweeten to taste. Simmer for 2–3 minutes until it reduces a little, stirring all the time, and then stir in the brandy or rum. Serve at once.

CHAPTER
6

*Basic recipes
& some
old favourites*

To FINISH: a patchwork of recipes. All the basics are here, from French dressing to homemade bread. I also decided to include some well loved dishes as suitable standbys for a lazy brunch or an early supper by the fire. These firm favourites can be made at short notice and provide the sort of comforting meal the Americans so aptly describe as Soul Food.

French dressing

The basic formula I use is 3 tablespoons oil to 1 vinegar. Having got the proportions right you can then add any number of different seasonings.

- Add a clove of garlic crushed with a little salt, black pepper, a teaspoon Dijon mustard and a little honey.
- Use a mixture of olive and sunflower oil for a lighter dressing.
- Substitute nut oil for the olive oil.
- Use different flavoured mustards.
- Instead of vinegar use lemon or lime juice: add it very gradually and taste to get the blend right.
- Add chopped fresh herbs, chopped chillies, or a combination of both.
- Soy sauce with a little chopped fresh ginger gives a delicious oriental dressing.
- Ketchup and Tabasco added to basic French dressing are delicious on bitter leaf salads.

Mayonnaise

2 egg yolks
1 scant tablespoon vinegar
1 teaspoon mild mustard
150 ml/¼ pint oil
salt and pepper

I always use a food processor for this sauce and add the oil slowly. I use a mixture of light and heavy olive oil.

Mix the yolk, vinegar and mustard in the food processor until well combined. While the motor is running, add the oil slowly, until the mixture thickens and you have a smooth glossy sauce. Season to taste with salt and pepper.

To this basic recipe you can add:

- Cloves of crushed garlic.
- Fresh herbs chopped directly into the mayonnaise in the processor once the oil has been added.
- A little tomato purée to give a delicate pink mayonnaise.
- You will find garlic mayonnaise on p. 148 and green mayonnaise on p. 163.

BASIC WHITE SAUCE

30 g/1 oz butter
30 g/1 oz plain flour
450 ml/¾ pint milk

This is a simple mixture of flour, butter and milk, to which you can add a variety of different flavourings, both sweet and savoury.

In a non-stick saucepan melt the butter and add the flour to make a roux. Mix in the milk, beating well and keeping the pan over a low heat.

Bring the sauce to the boil and simmer for 2–3 minutes. The sauce should be glossy and smooth and no taste of raw flour should remain.

Here are some variations.

☐ Cheese sauce: add 60–85 g/2–3 oz grated cheese, 1 teaspoon ready made mustard and a little paprika.

☐ Mustard sauce: add 1–2 tablespoons wholegrain mustard.

☐ Savoury lemon sauce: add the grated zest and juice of a small lemon, salt and pepper and some chopped fresh chives.

☐ Sauce for fish: substitute 300 ml/½ pint fish stock and 150 ml/¼ pint cream for the milk, and add a little tomato purée.

☐ Mushroom sauce: fry 60 g/2 oz sliced mushrooms in a little extra butter and add to the basic sauce mix with a little lemon juice or dry sherry.

☐ Sweet sauces: add 1–2 tablespoons caster sugar and either lemon juice, vanilla, brandy or orange liqueur to taste.

REAL CUSTARD

yolks of 3 eggs
2–3 tablespoons caster sugar
1 scant tablespoon cornflour
450 ml/¾ pint creamy milk
1 vanilla pod, or ½ teaspoon vanilla essence

Mix the egg yolks, sugar and cornflour to a smooth paste, adding a little milk if necessary. Bring the remaining milk to the boil and remove from the heat. If you have time place a vanilla pod in the milk and allow it to infuse for 15 minutes, remove the pod and reheat the milk. Alternatively, add the vanilla essence.

Mix a little hot milk with the eggs etc. and then add the remaining milk. Strain the custard into a clean saucepan and simmer over a very gentle heat for 1–2 minutes, until thick and no taste of raw cornflour remains.

Real gravy

pan scrapings and fat from the joint
about 1 tablespoon flour
450 ml/¾ pint light stock or vegetable
  water
salt, pepper

I usually place a chopped onion in the pan when I am roasting meat: the onion caramelizes and this gives both a wonderful flavour and colour to the gravy.

Pour off as much fat from the pan as possible and sprinkle on the flour. Place the roasting pan over a medium heat and stir the flour into the remaining fat, scraping up all the bits. Slowly pour on the stock and continue to mix, stirring all the time, until the gravy thickens. Strain into a clean pan and correct the seasoning. Simmer until the gravy is the correct thickness.

Tomato coulis

1 shallot, finely chopped
1 tablespoon olive oil
1–2 plump cloves garlic
450 g/1 lb ripe tomatoes, chopped
  (tinned as a last resort)
salt and pepper
fresh herbs to taste

Fry the shallot in the oil until soft. Crush and add the garlic and cook for 60 seconds. Add the tomatoes and a little black pepper and salt. I like to add a few sprigs of fresh oregano or thyme at this stage. Bring the mixture to a simmer and cook until the tomatoes are very soft. Pass through a Mouli or sieve and then return the sauce to the heat, reducing if necessary to thicken.

CREOLE SEASONING

1 tablespoon fennel seeds
1 tablespoon dried thyme
1 tablespoon dried sage
2 tablespoons dried onion flakes
2 tablespoons garlic salt
1 tablespoon black peppercorns
1 teaspoon cayenne pepper
2 tablespoons paprika

Place the whole spices in a well cleaned coffee grinder and whizz until finely powdered. Add the paprika and cayenne, mix and store in an airtight tin until needed.

BREAD

725 g/1½ lb strong flour
1 teaspoon salt
1 packet easyblend yeast
2 tablespoons vegetable oil
about 450 ml/¾ pint warm water

I often make bread as I find it wonderfully soothing after a heavy day. This simple recipe can be endlessly adapted. You can make bread richer by adding fat, milk and eggs, but all these and sugar too will inhibit the yeast, so add extra to compensate. For a rich sweet egg loaf I use double the yeast that I put into my basic recipe.

Mix the flour, salt and yeast together then add the oil and the water. Stir well. The mixture should be soft but not sticky, and as flours vary it is difficult to be precise about the amount of water needed.

Turn the dough on to a lightly floured board and knead for 5 minutes. An electric mixer with a dough hook or a food processor can be used. Cover the ball of dough with a damp cloth and put to rise until doubled in size. I use the airing cupboard.

Knock back the dough and shape into whatever form you like. You can use this dough to make a loaf of bread, small rolls, pizza bases and flat loaves to cook over hot coals on the barbecue.

Once shaped, allow the dough to rise for a second time, again covered with a damp cloth. Bake in a hot oven, 230°C/450°F/Gas 8. The time varies depending on the size of loaf you are making. Rolls may take 10 minutes and a large loaf about 30 minutes. Test the bread by tapping the base of the loaf: if done the bread should sound hollow.

SPONGE CAKE

115 g/4 oz butter
115 g/4 oz sugar
2 eggs (approximate weight 115 g/4 oz)
115 g/4 oz self-raising flour

Basic sponge cake is a very simple and useful standby. Add a variety of bits to it and you have anything from a cherry cake to an iced lemon bun!

I use a food processor to make the mixture. I realize that the texture is not cake-competition perfect, but then this cake is for eating not showing.

Use the weight of the eggs in caster sugar, butter (or margarine) and self-raising flour.

I never make more than a 4-egg quantity at one time, as it only takes moments to whip up the sponge batter and large quantities can be tricky to handle.

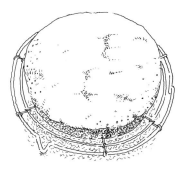

Place the butter and sugar in the food processor fitted with its metal blade and whizz until pale and creamy. With the motor running, add the eggs one at a time. Remember to break the eggs into a cup first, not only to check for freshness but to make quite sure no egg shell falls in accidentally. Picking tiny bits of egg shell from half-made cake mixture is neither quick nor amusing.

When the eggs have been added, stop the motor and add the flour all at once. If you are making a flavoured cake add the flavourings at this point too. Replace the processor lid, but leave open the feed tube. In short bursts, mix the flour into the eggs. This will only take a few moments. Pour into prepared tins.

Cook the sponge in a medium oven, at 180°C/360°F/Gas 4, until the cake is risen, golden brown and springy to the touch. A cooked sponge will start to pull from the side of the tin, and this is a good sign that it is ready. Don't run the risk of the cake sinking in the centre by prodding it too soon with a skewer.

The cooking time will vary depending on the size of tin used, but two sandwich tins filled with a 3-egg mixture will take 20–25 minutes, little cup cakes will take 12–15 minutes, and a loaf tin filled with a 4-egg mixture may take up to 1 hour.

Shortcrust pastry

225 g/8 oz butter
30 g/1 oz lard
450 g/1 lb plain flour
pinch salt
1 egg
cold water

I always make my pastry with butter, as I don't eat pies too often and love the flavour of rich buttery pastry when I do. For preference I use concentrated cooking butter, which is usually less costly than other butter and keeps well in the freezer. I always make pastry in batches to use 450 g/1 lb of flour, and freeze any I don't need at once.

Use a food processor for perfect results each time.

Cut the cold fats into small cubes and place with the flour and salt in the food processor bowl. Use a metal blade to cut the fat into the flour until the mixture really does resemble cake or breadcrumbs. I then tip the mixture into a large mixing bowl. While you can add the egg and water in the processor I find adding it by hand gives a more predictable result.

Beat the egg with about 4 tablespoons of water, sprinkle over the flour mixture and cut it in with a knife. If the mixture does not want to hold together, add a little more water. Once it starts to stick use your hands to quickly and lightly knead it into a ball. Wrap in polythene and leave to rest in a cool place for 30 minutes.

For a sweet flan pastry, I add 1 tablespoon each of cornflour and icing sugar to the original recipe.

Choux pastry

75 g/2½ oz plain flour
pinch salt
150 ml/¼ pint water
60 g/2 oz butter
2 size 3 eggs, beaten

Sift the flour and salt together and set aside. In a heavy saucepan heat the water with the butter until the butter has melted. Bring the mixture to a full rolling boil and then, all at once, tip in the flour. Beat well with a wooden spoon, and as soon as the mixture forms a ball, remove from the heat.

Continue to beat a few moments longer and then allow to cool for 5 minutes. Add the beaten egg a little at a time, beating well until you have a glossy, but still quite stiff paste. Cover with a damp cloth until needed.

I usually add the egg in the food processor, especially when I am adding other ingredients to make beignets (p. 82).

Fish cakes

serves 4–6
450 g/1 lb old potatoes, peeled
1 size 2 egg, beaten
salt and pepper
170–225 g/6–8 oz fish
chopped herbs, optional
oil for frying

I make these fish cakes with tinned tuna or salmon, but fresh salmon or smoked haddock would be very good.

Boil and mash the potatoes, then beat in the egg. Season well and mix in the flaked fish. You can add some chopped chervil, dill or parsley if you like.

Shape the mixture into flat cakes, and fry a few at a time in oil in a large frying pan, until golden on both sides, about 15 minutes.

Soft roes on toast

per person
1 slice hot toast
115 g/4 oz fresh soft herring roes
a little beaten egg, seasoned with salt
  and pepper
fresh white breadcrumbs
butter for frying
lemon wedges, to serve

Wash the roes and pat dry. Dip into the egg and then the breadcrumbs.

Melt the butter in a frying pan and fry the roes over a moderate heat until the coating is crisp. Don't worry if they crumble, just spoon everything on to the toast and top with a squeeze of lemon.

HERRINGS FRIED IN OATMEAL

per person
1 large fresh herring
salt, pepper
a handful medium oatmeal
butter, for frying
lemon wedges, to serve

Season the cleaned fish well and pat on the oatmeal to coat. Fry in hot butter for 4–5 minutes each side. Serve with lemon.

SMOKED HADDOCK SOUFFLÉ

serves 4–6
340 g/12 oz smoked haddock, poached in 300 ml/½ pint milk
60 g/2 oz butter
1 small onion, finely chopped
1 heaped teaspoon ground cumin
60 g/2 oz flour
4 egg yolks
black pepper
4 or 5 egg whites
butter and breadcrumbs, to line the dish

Butter the inside of a soufflé dish and sprinkle with breadcrumbs.

Melt the butter and fry the onion until golden. Add the cumin and fry for 30 seconds, then add the flour. Make a sauce, using the strained fish liquor. Boil for 2–3 minutes, then allow to cool slightly. Beat the yolks into the sauce one at a time and then add some black pepper (the salt in the fish should be sufficient). Stir in the flaked, skinned and boned fish.

Beat the egg whites until stiff and fold them in carefully. Pour into the prepared dish and bake in a preheated oven, at 200°C/400°F/Gas 6, for 30–35 minutes. The soufflé should be slightly soft in the middle.

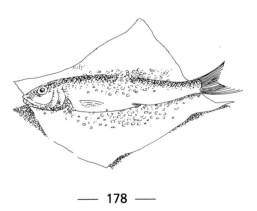

BACON & MUSHROOM RISOTTO

serves 4
30 g/1 oz dried porcini mushrooms
1 medium onion, chopped
2 tablespoons olive oil
60 g/2 oz butter
1 clove garlic, finely chopped
**115 g/4 oz lean back bacon or pancetta,
  cut into pieces**
600 ml/1 pint light stock
285 g/10 oz risotto rice
8 tablespoons white wine
**60 g/2 oz Parmesan cheese, freshly
  grated**

Soak the dried mushrooms in 300 ml/½ pint warm water for 30 minutes. Fry the onion in the oil and half the butter until pale and golden, then add the garlic. Drain the mushrooms, reserving the soaking liquid, and chop. Add them to the onion with the bacon and cook, stirring, for 60 seconds.

Strain the mushroom soaking liquid into the stock and put this to boil in another saucepan.

Put the rice into the onion mixture and stir for 60 seconds until well coated with butter, then add the wine and boil for 2 minutes until absorbed.

Add the stock, a little at a time, stirring while it is absorbed, until the rice is cooked, 15–18 minutes. The rice should still have a bite and there should be a little sauce surrounding it. You may not need all the stock.

Remove from the heat and stir in the remaining butter and Parmesan, taste and correct seasoning and leave to settle for 2–3 minutes before serving.

Note: leftover risotto can be shaped into small balls and deep-fried. This is delicious as a canapé or with salad.

KEDGEREE

serves 4–6
450 g/1 lb smoked cod or haddock
bay leaf
60 g/2 oz butter
1 small onion, finely chopped
1 teaspoon ground cumin
1 teaspoon ground coriander
½ teaspoon turmeric
225 g/8 oz long-grain rice
150 ml/¼ pint single cream
2–3 hardboiled eggs, quartered
½ teaspoon garam masala

Poach the fish in water to cover with a bay leaf. Remove the fish, reserving the liquid. Flake the fish, removing all skin and bone, and reserve. Strain the liquid and make up to 600 ml/ 1 pint.

In a large saucepan, melt the butter and fry the onion until soft. Add the spices and fry, stirring all the time, for 60 seconds. Add the rice and continue to cook, stirring, for a further 2 minutes.

Add the water, bring to the boil, cover and simmer for 20 minutes until the rice is cooked, adding more water if necessary. Toss the rice with a fork and add the fish.

Meanwhile, warm the cream over a gentle heat. Taste the rice to check seasoning, adjust as necessary, then tip on to a serving dish and pour over the warm cream. Arrange the eggs on top, sprinkle on the garam masala and serve at once.

TWICE-BAKED CHEESE SOUFFLÉ

serves 6
85 g/3 oz butter
85 g/3 oz plain flour
300 ml /½ pint milk
4 size 2 eggs, separated
1 teaspoon mustard
salt and pepper
**115 g/4 oz strong Cheddar cheese,
   grated**
60 g/2 oz Parmesan cheese

to finish
300 ml/½ pint single cream
chopped chives

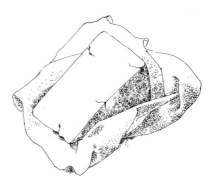

*This is a recipe given to me by Bob
Payton, in whose beautiful hotel,
Stapleford Park, I first ate these twice-
baked soufflés. A real treat, they are
made the day before needed, then
simply reheated with a little cream
poured over.*

*For a change, I love a spoonful of
pesto stirred in with the cheese mixture,
and perhaps a few chopped sun-dried
tomatoes as well. If you do this, you
could cut the total amount of cheese
back to 115 g/4 oz.*

Heat the oven to 150°C/300°F/Gas 2.

Make a thick white sauce by melting
the butter, adding the flour and then
beating in the milk. Boil the sauce for
3–4 minutes, until thick and no raw
flour taste remains.

Allow to cool, then stir in the egg
yolks one at a time. Add the mustard
and season well with salt and pepper
before stirring in both types of cheese.

Whisk the egg whites until stiff and
fold into the cheese mixture. Divide the
mixture between six well greased
10 cm/4 inch soufflé dishes.

Cook the soufflés in the hot oven, in
2.5 cm/1 inch boiling water in a baking
dish, for 25 minutes, or until well risen
and beginning to brown.

Remove from the oven and allow to
cool for 5 minutes, then turn on to a
large ovenproof dish. Cover and store
in the fridge until needed.

When ready to serve, heat the oven to
190°C/380°F/Gas 5, pour the cream
over the soufflés and cook for 10
minutes. Sprinkle with chopped chives.

Baked cheese & egg casserole

serves 4
3 slices white bread, toasted
115 g/4 oz Cheddar cheese, grated
4 size 3 eggs, beaten
450 ml/¾ pint milk
½ teaspoon salt
½ teaspoon prepared mustard
black pepper

This recipe comes from a friend in Louisiana. It must be made the night before it's needed to allow the bread to soak up the custard. Serve with crisply grilled bacon.

Cut the bread into small squares and arrange in a well greased ovenproof dish. Mix the remaining ingredients together and pour over the bread. Put in the fridge overnight.

Heat the oven to 160°C/325°F/Gas 3, and bake the dish for 30–40 minutes, or until golden and crisp on top.

Bubble & squeak

serves 6
1 tablespoon goose fat, bacon fat or oil
725 g/1½ lb mashed potato
225 g/8 oz cold cooked spring greens or Savoy cabbage
salt and pepper
1 small onion, chopped

Serve this with fried eggs and bacon or cold meat and chutney.

Melt the fat in a pan and fry the onion until transparent. Add the potato and cabbage, stirring to break up any lumps. Season well with salt and pepper and continue to fry over a medium heat, allowing the mixture to crisp on the bottom before turning. Remember it's the crispy bits that are delicious, so don't rush.

GRATIN OF POTATOES, TOMATOES & MOZZARELLA

serves 4–6
450 g/1 lb waxy potatoes, peeled
3 large beef tomatoes, sliced
225 g/8 oz mozzarella cheese, sliced
1–2 tablespoons olive oil
basil leaves
salt, black pepper

Parboil the potatoes for about 5 minutes, then allow to cool and cut into 5 mm/¼ inch slices.

Brush a gratin dish with a little oil and arrange alternate slices of potato, tomato, and cheese, overlapping in rings around the dish, and tucking in a basil leaf occasionally. Drizzle the remaining oil over the top and season with a little salt and black pepper.

Bake in a preheated oven, at 180°C/360°F/Gas 4, for 30 minutes, until the potatoes are cooked and the cheese has browned.

RÖSTI

serves 4–6
450 g/1 lb potatoes, peeled
115 g/4 oz streaky bacon
2 tablespoons oil
1 medium onion, sliced
1 tablespoon butter

This potato dish comes from Switzerland. Serve it with fried eggs or sliced ham.

Put the potatoes in a pan of cold water and bring to the boil. Cook for 5 minutes and drain. The potatoes should be firm but not raw.

While the potatoes cool, cut the bacon into fine strips and fry in a heavy based frying pan in the oil until crisp. Remove from the pan, leaving in as much fat as possible, and fry the onions. When the onions are beginning to brown, remove from the pan, again leaving as much fat as possible.

Grate the cooled potatoes, on the coarsest side of the grater, into a large bowl, and combine them with the onion and bacon, seasoning well. I find it easiest to mix carefully with my hands.

Add the butter to the pan and melt over a medium heat. Put in the potato mixture and pat down lightly to form a large cake. Fry over a medium/low heat for 10 minutes. The underside should be golden.

Find a plate that fits just into the pan, slip a palette knife around under the cake, and invert it on to the plate. If necessary melt a little more butter in the pan, then fry the other side until golden.

TOAD IN THE HOLE

serves 4
8 pork sausages
2 tablespoons lard or oil

for the batter
2 eggs
140 g/5 oz plain flour
salt and pepper
300 ml/½ pint milk
½ teaspoon dried mixed herbs

This is a good example of a recipe where choosing the best ingredients makes such a difference to the finished dish. I like coarse meaty sausages with a few herbs added.

Make the batter using the eggs, flour and milk, and season well with salt, pepper and the herbs. Leave to stand for a few minutes.

Heat the oven to 200°C/400°F/Gas 6, and roast the sausages for 10 minutes in a large ovenproof dish in the lard or oil.

Remove the dish from the oven, pour in the batter and continue to cook for a further 30–40 minutes, until the pudding is fluffy and golden brown. Serve at once.

CORNED BEEF HASH

serves 4–6
1 large Spanish onion, chopped
2–3 tablespoons oil
1 plump clove garlic, finely chopped
1 large tin corned beef, chopped
450 g/1 lb cooked potato
salt, pepper
Tabasco

Fry the onion in oil in a large pan until soft and beginning to colour. Add the garlic, beef and potato, and stir everything together, seasoning well with salt, pepper and Tabasco. Allow the mixture to crisp on the bottom, then turn and cook the other side.

INDEX